FREQUENTLY ASKED CODING INTERVIEW

Part 1: Core Java

Rajini Adhikesavan

Copyright © 2017 by Rajini Adhikesavan

All rights reserved. No portion of this book may be reproduced in any form without permission from the publisher, except as permitted by U.S. copyright law.

Second Edition

Clear Pebble LLC
Sacramento, CA

To family, friends and teachers

PREFACE

Who are the intended audience?

This book provides frequently asked coding interview questions and answers for programmers preparing for job interviews. These questions and answers are intended for programmers and students with some java programming experience and are not for beginners who are just starting to learn programming. Java programmers can review and learn Core Java Basic and Advanced concepts in preparation for a job interview.

Why this book?

There are many books and online tutorials available for coding interview preparation, but they are exhaustive in volume and content. This book provides concise and clear material on important topics that can be reviewed in a short period of time.

These coding questions and answers have been compiled from personal study materials collected over 15 years after interviewing with hundreds of silicon valley companies. After receiving positive feedback from friends and colleagues who successfully used this material to land a job, it has been compiled to the current format.

This is a sincere attempt to make coding interview preparation as simple and easy as possible.

What's in this book?

This book has simplified and distilled collection of frequently asked coding interview questions and answers along with basic concepts.

Part 1 covers Core Java Programming. Part 2 covers Java Algorithms and Data Structures. Core Java Programming package has 200+

questions. There are 140+ questions in Algorithms and Data Structures.

How can I best use this book ?

Spending time on each question, answer, and answer explanation as well as going through the details thoroughly will ensure a complete understanding of the concepts covered.

Since many of the questions in specific categories are related, working on them together helps in a comprehensive coverage of related concepts.

Can I use this book to prepare for interviews with Google, Facebook or Amazon?

These coding interview questions and answers are designed for comprehensive coverage of important topics in core java basic and advanced concepts. The material is designed to be concise and clear providing one simple and efficient solution for a coding problem, although a problem can be solved using different methods.

Several topics and concepts have been broken down into smaller units with a clear solution and explanation. These concepts and solutions can be put together to solve similar or larger problems.

These coding interview questions and answers are designed for users to be able to review and master frequently asked questions in any software company.

Rajini Adhikesavan
San Francisco, CA
July, 2024

CONTENTS

CORE JAVA BASICS

1 Basic Programming Structures and Operations
   1.1 DataTypes, Assignments and Operators   1
   1.2 String   7

2 Classes, Objects and Methods
   2.1 Methods, Constructors and Access Modifiers   15
   2.2 final, finalize and finally   25
   2.3 Static fields and initialization blocks   29

3 Object-Oriented Concepts
   3.1 Inheritance and Composition   35
   3.2 Abstract Class and Interface   44
   3.3 Cloneable Interface   51
   3.4 Inner Classes   55
   3.5 Runtime Type Identification   60

4 Exceptions, Input Streams and Serialization
   4.1 Exception Hierarchy   63
   4.2 Error and Runtime Exception   65
   4.3 Try and Catch   69
   4.4 File Input and Output Streams   73
   4.5 Object Serialization   75

5 Language Features
   5.1 Generics   83
   5.2 Annotation   86
   5.3 Enum Types   88

CORE JAVA ADVANCED

6 Collections
6.1 Collection Framework Basics	92
6.2 Arrays, ArrayList and LinkedList	95
6.3 HashSet, HashMap and Concurrent HashMap	102
6.4 hashCode and equals	110
6.5 TreeSet and TreeMap	120
6.6 Views and Wrappers	127
6.7 Collection Algorithms	135

7 Threads
7.1 Thread Basics	138
7.2 Thread Demo and sleep	142
7.3 Runnable interface and interrupt	150
7.4 Thread Priorities and yield	161
7.5 Concurrency Basics	165
7.6 Concurrency and Synchronization	174
7.7 Deadlocks, Wait and Notify	184

8 JDBC
8.1 JDBC Basics	200
8.2 Statement, Query and Transactions	203

9 Design Patterns
9.1 Creational Patterns	208
9.2 Structural Patterns	217
9.3 Behavioral Patterns	223

10 JVM Architecture
10.1 JVM Basics	237
10.2 Garbage Collection	243

CORE JAVA BASICS

Basic Programming Structures and Operations

1.1 DATATYPES, ASSIGNMENTS AND OPERATORS

1.1.1

Length of the primitive data types in Java are as follows:

1. short – 2 bytes
2. int and float – 4 bytes
3. long and double – 8 bytes

Which of the above are correct?

a. 1 and 2
b. 1, 2, and 3
c. 2 and 3
d. None of the above

Ans: b

Answer Explanation:

Primitive data types are byte, short, int, long, double and float.

All six data types are made up of bytes with 8 bits and the left most bit is used to represent the sign. In the sign bit, 0 represents positive and 1 represents negative. Rest of the bits represent the value using two's complement notation.

Type	Bytes	Bits	Min	Max
byte	1	8	-2^7	$2^7 - 1$
short	2	16	-2^{15}	$2^{15} - 1$
int	4	32	-2^{31}	$2^{31} - 1$
long	8	64	-2^{63}	$2^{63} - 1$
float	4	32	N/A	N/A
double	8	64	N/A	N/A

With 1 byte (8 bit) there are 256 (2^8) possible numbers. Since the left most is the sign bit, total possible numbers for one byte becomes 2^7.

The positive range is one less than the negative because 0 is stored as a positive number.

1.1.2

In Java, char is

a. 1 byte
b. 2 bytes
c. 4 bytes
d. 8 bytes

Ans: b

Answer Explanation:

In Java, char is a 2 byte or 16 bit Unicode character. It has a minimum value of 0 and maximum value of $2^{16} -1$. The range is one less because 0 is stored as a positive number.

1.1.3

When 'double' is type casted to 'int' as shown below

double value = 7.89999;
int val = (int) value; // type-cast

a. Information may be lost during type-cast
b. Information is never lost during type-cast
c. Information is always lost during type-cast
d. None of the above.

Ans: a

Answer Explanation:

Primitive values can be converted from one type to another using casting. Casts can be implicit or explicit casts.

DATATYPES, ASSIGNMENTS AND OPERATORS

Implicit cast happens when a smaller type is converted to a larger type, for example short to a double.

If a larger type is converted into a smaller type, for example from double to int as below, an explicit cast is needed. If explicit cast is not added, it results in a compiler error.

double value = 7.89999;
int val = value; // compiler-error

gives a compiler error
Type mismatch: cannot convert from double to int

This needs an explicit cast as
int val = (int) value; // type-cast

1.1.4

What's the best way to round the following floating point number x to the nearest integer?

double x = 9.998;

a. int y = (int) x;
b. int y = x;
c. int y = (int) Math.round(x);
d. int y = (int) new Double(x).intValue();

Ans: c

Answer Explanation:

public static void main(String [] args) {

    double x = 9.998;
    int a = (int) x;
    int b = (int) new Double(x).intValue();
    int y = (int) Math.*round*(x);

    System.*out*.println("Value of a is: " + a);
    System.*out*.println("Value of b is: " + b);

System.*out*.println("Value of y after Math.round(x) is: " + y);
}

Output:

Value of a is: 9
Value of b is: 9
Value of y after Math.round(x) is: 10

Casting to int or converting using intValue() truncates the decimals, while Math.round() functionality rounds the number to the closest integer.

1.1.5

What will be the values of m and n in the following code?

int x = 4;
int y = 4;
int m = 5 * ++x;
int n = 5 * y++;

a. m=20 and n=25
b. m=25 and n=25
c. m=20 and n=20
d. m=25 and n=20

Ans: d

Answer Explanation:

public static void main(String [] args) {
    int x = 4;
    int y = 4;
    int m = 5 * ++x;
    int n = 5 * y++;

    System.*out*.println("Value of m is: " + m);
    System.*out*.println("Value of n is: " + n);
}

Output:

Value of m is: 25
Value of n is: 20

Prefix and postfix increment operators are used for incrementing a variable in an expression. Prefix operator increments the variable before the expression is evaluated, while the postfix operator increments the value after the expression is evaluated.

In the above sample, ++x increments 4 to 5 and the result is 25 while y++ does not increment the value so the result of the expression is 20. After the expression is evaluated, y is incremented to 5 because of the postfix operator. Same rules apply for the prefix and postfix decrement operators also.

1.1.6

Which of the following data type is a good choice for handling currencies?

a. float
b. double
c. class BigInteger
d. class BigDecimal

Ans: d

Answer Explanation:

public static void main(String [] args) {

    BigDecimal price = **new** BigDecimal("99.99");
    BigDecimal discountPercent = **new** BigDecimal("0.10");

    BigDecimal discount = price.multiply(discountPercent);
    BigDecimal salePrice = price.subtract(discount);
    salePrice = salePrice.setScale(2, BigDecimal.*ROUND_HALF_UP*);

    System.*out*.println("Original price is: " + price);

```
        System.out.println("Sale price is: " + salePrice );
}
```

Output:

Original price is: 99.99
Sale price is: 89.99

The above program demonstrates using BigDecimal for handling currencies. BigDecimal provides functionality for arithmetic operations and rounding with different rounding modes.

1.2 STRING

1.2.1

String str = "hello";

In the above initiation, str is a

a. string variable
b. string object
c. string literal
d. all of the above

Ans: a

Answer Explanation:

The above declaration creates a string literal "hello". String literal is an instance of the class String, which is also a String object.

A String object with value "hello" is created on the heap and the address to the location is returned to str. So, str is a string variable which stores the location of the String object with value "hello".

1.2.2

1. String a = "hello";
2. String b = new String("hello");

In the above code snippet, first initiation is a more efficient way of creating a String object than the second one, because

a. The second initiation does not create a string literal
b. The second initiation creates a string literal
c. The second initiation creates a string object
d. The second initiation creates a string literal followed by another string object

Ans: d

Answer Explanation:

String a = "hello";
String b = new String("hello");

In the first initialization above, a string literal is created. A string literal is an instance of the class String. In the second initialization also a string literal is created, followed by creation of a String object with the same value.

In the above initiations, a == b returns false, since both strings have the same value but are not referencing the same memory location.

String a = "hello";
String b = "hello";

In the above initiations, a==b returns true, as both the strings are referencing the same memory location.

Every time a string literal is created as above, the intern() method on this String object is invoked. This method references the internal pool of String objects maintained by the String class.

If the string that called intern() is already present in the pool, a reference to that object is returned. If the string is not present, then a new string object is added to the pool and the reference is returned.

1.2.3

String str1 = "hello";
String str2 = " sunshine!";

str1 = str1.concat(str2);
str2 = str2.substring(1,4);

System.*out*.println("str1: " + str1);
System.*out*.println("str2: " + str2);

The above code snippet gives the following output:
str1: hello sunshine!
str2: sun

As the String class is immutable, once a String object is created it cannot be changed. How was it possible to change the strings str1 and str2 to different values from their original values "hello" and "sunshine"?

a. String objects can be changed
b. The methods create and return a new string object
c. Strings are not constant
d. All of the above

Ans: b

Answer Explanation:

In java, String object's individual character sequence cannot be changed. Since the individual characters in a Java string cannot be changed, the String class is called immutable.

Contents of the string variables like str1 and str2 can be changed and made to refer to a different string. Strings are on the heap and a string variable is just a pointer to the String object in the heap.

String object is constant and cannot be changed. Methods like concat and substring in the String class just create a new String object and return the values.

1.2.4

```
String str1 = "meadow";
String str2 = "meadow";

if(str1 == str2) {
      System.out.println("Equal");
} else {
      System.out.println("Unequal");
}
```

What would be the output of the above program?

a. Equal
b. Unequal

c. Equal or Unequal
d. None of the above

Ans: a

Answer Explanation:

In the above case, a==b returns true as both the strings are referencing the same memory location. Every time a string literal is created as above, the intern() method on this String object is invoked. This method references the internal pool of String objects maintained by the String class.

If the string that called intern() is already present in the pool, a reference to this object is returned. If the string is not present, then a new string object is added to the pool and the reference is returned.

1.2.5

String str1 = "abc";
String str2 = String.*valueOf*(str1);
str1==str2 returns

a. true
b. false

Ans: a

Answer Explanation:

String.valueOf() method is used for converting integer and character arrays to String. When String object is passed as an argument it returns the reference to the same String object.

char val [] = {'a','b', 'c', 'd', 'e'};
String str = String.*valueOf*(val);

In the above snippet, str is a String object that is created from a char array.

1.2.6

String s = "Hello";
s = s + " sunshine,";
s = s + " how";
s = s + " are";
s = s + " you?";

StringBuilder sb = **new** StringBuilder("Hello");
sb.append(" sunshine,").append(" how").append(" are").append(" you?");

In the above code snippet, how many new objects are created while appending to string s and then for appending to StringBuilder sb?

a. 5 and 5
b. 5 and 1
c. 1 and 5
d. none of the above

Ans: b

Answer Explanation:

String s = "Hello";
s = s + " sunshine";

In line 2 of the above code snippet, when the string object is appended to another string literal, a new String object is created appending the two strings.

As the original String object is immutable, it cannot be changed, so a new String object is created for every concat operation. Because of this, for operations having several string concatenations, multiple String objects are created which is not efficient.

Meanwhile, in line 2 of the code snippet below, a string is appended to the original StringBuilder object. This is possible since StringBuilder class is mutable.

StringBuilder sb = **new** StringBuilder("Hello");
sb.append(" sunshine,");

So, for concatenating large number of strings, StringBuilder is more efficient than String.

1.2.7

StringBuffer performs slower than StringBuilder because StringBuffer is

a. Synchronized
b. Mutable
c. Transient
d. All of the above

Ans: a

Answer Explanation:

All the public methods of StringBuffer are synchronized that makes it thread-safe, this also makes using this class slower than using StringBuilder.

Since String is immutable, it's automatically thread-safe. StringBuilder and StringBuffer are both mutable but only StringBuffer is thread-safe.

1.2.8

String jsonStr = "firstName:'Tom',lastName:'Sawyer',age:13";

Which of the following will be the best option to split the above string using comma as delimiter?

a. String.split
b. StringTokenizer
c. StringBuffer
d. StringBuilder

Ans: a

AnswerExplanation:

```java
public static void main(String [] args) {

    String jsonStr = "firstName:'Tom',lastName:'Sawyer',age:13";
    String [] tokens = jsonStr.split(",");

    for(String token : tokens) {
        System.out.println(token);
    }
}
```

Output:

firstName:'Tom'
lastName:'Sawyer'
age:13

The above program prints the tokens after splitting the comma delimited json string. The beginning and closing braces have been removed from the json string for simplicity.

StringTokenizer can also be used for this operation, but according to the Java documentation.

"StringTokenizer is a legacy class that is retained for compatibility reasons although its use is discouraged in new code. It is recommended that anyone seeking this functionality use the split method of String or the java.util.regex package instead."

1.2.9

```java
String str1 = "meadow";
String str2 = "meadow";

if(str1 == str2) {
    System.out.println("str1==str2 is true");
}

if(str1.equals(str2)) {
    System.out.println("str1.equals(str2) is true");
}
```

Difference between == and .equals() operator in String is

a. == operator and .equals() method both compare the content.
b. == operator and .equals() method both compare the memory location.
c. == operator compares the contents and .equals() method compare the memory location.
d. == operator compares the memory location and .equals() method compares the content.

Ans: d

Answer Explanation:

== checks if the String objects compared are referring to same memory location, while .equals() operator checks if the content of two strings are same.

.equals() method of the Object class compares if the two objects are referring to the same memory address. This method is overridden by the String class to compare the contents of the String objects.

Output:

str1==str2 is true
str1.equals(str2) is true

Classes, Objects and Methods

2.1 METHODS, CONSTRUCTORS AND ACCESS MODIFIERS

2.1.1

Which of the following definitions regarding Class and Object are correct?

1. A Class is a template that defines the state and behavior of its objects.
2. Object is an instance of the Class that has its own states and behaviors.
3. Object's state depends on the values defined for its instance variables.
4. Object's behavior is determined by the methods that have the logic to manipulate the data.

a. 1 and 2
b. 3 and 4
c. 1, 2 and 3
d. All of the above

Ans: d

Answer Explanation:

Class is a blueprint from which individual objects are created. Instance variables are declared within the class but outside any method.

```
public class Aircraft {

    private String name;

    public Aircraft(String n) {
        name = n;
    }

    public void fly() {
        System.out.println("Prepare to fly");
    }
}
```

The above code snippet declares a class Airplane with instance variable name and method fly.

Aircraft(String n) is the constructor. Constructor has the same name as the class and no return value.

public static void main(String [] args) {

    Aircraft aircraft = new Aircraft("Boeing 727");
}

In the above declaration, aircraft object is created using the new key word, aircraft object is an instance of the class Aircraft. The constructor declared above, Aircraft(String n) with a String parameter is used for creating the aircraft object.

2.1.2

Aircraft jet = new Aircraft();
Aircraft plane = jet;

jet.startEngine();
plane.stopEngine();

The above code:

a. Will invoke startEngine() and stopEngine() on the same aircraft, since both object variables refer to the same object.
b. Will invoke startEngine() and stopEngine() on two different aircrafts, since both object variables refer to different objects.
c. One object variable cannot be assigned to another.
d. None of the above.

Ans: a

Answer Explanation:

In the above example, Aircraft object jet is created first, and then another object plane is created and assigned to jet. Now, both jet and plane are referring to the same object.

When jet.startEngine() is called, the method on this object is invoked and when plane.stopEngine() is called later, the stopEngine method on the same object is invoked.

2.1.3

In the code snippet below, both method 1 and method 2 are modifying startTime that is passed as method parameter

method 1:

```
public static void setAircraftStartTime(Date startTime,
                                        int delayedHours)
{
    long startTimeInMillisec = startTime.getTime();
    long delayInMillisec = delayedHours * 60 * 60 * 1000L;

    startTime = new Date(startTimeInMillisec + delayInMillisec);
}
```

method 2:

```
public static void setAircraftStartTime(Date startTime,
                                        int delayedHours)
{
    long startTimeInMillisec = startTime.getTime();
    long delayInMillisec = delayedHours * 60 * 60 * 1000L;

    startTime.setTime(startTimeInMillisec + delayInMillisec);
}
```

a. Both method 1 and method 2 will change the startTime passed as method parameter.
b. Method 1 will not change the startTime value.
c. Method 2 will not change the startTime value.
d. None of the above.

Ans: b

Answer Explanation:

An object variable passed into a method is passed by reference. Actually it's the copy of the reference variable. In this example, it's startTime.

Both, calling method and the called method have a copy of the same reference variable and refer to the same object on the heap. When the object is modified inside the called method2 as startTime.setTime(..), the calling method will also see the change, as both are referring to the same object.

However the called method1 cannot change the object reference variable startTime by assigning a new object as startTime= **new** Date(..). This is because, when the method returns, the calling method will be still referring to the original object.

String argument passed into a method also cannot be changed by assigning a new value for the same reason. When a primitive type like int is passed to a method, it's passed by value, and also cannot be changed inside the method by assignment.

Array values passed as parameter into a method can be changed by assigning new values inside the method since Array values are passed by reference.

2.1.4

A constructor

1. has the same name as the class.
2. may take one or more parameters.
3. is always called with a new keyword.
4. has no return value.

Which of the above statements are true?

a. 1, 3, and 4
b. 1 and 2
c. All of the above
d. None of the above

Ans: c

Answer Explanation:

```
public class Airplane {

    private String name;

    public void fly() {
        System.out.println("Prepare to fly");
    }
}
```

The above code snippet defines a class Airplane, with instance variable name and method fly(). An object can be created using the new keyword. The new keyword is followed by call to a constructor which initializes the object.

Aircraft aircraft = new Aircraft();

Since no constructor was defined in the class, the default, no argument constructor generated by the compiler was used.

If a constructor is specified in the class with an argument, then the no argument constructor will not be generated by the compiler. In this scenario, if a no argument constructor is needed, it has to be added manually. Constructors can also be explicitly defined as follows:

```
public class Aircraft {

    private String name;

    public Aircraft() {
        // default constructor automatically created by compiler,
        // if no constructors are defined
    }
    public Aircraft(String n) {
```

```
        name = n;
    }
    public void fly() {
        System.out.println("Prepare to fly");
    }
}
```

Aircraft() and Aircraft(String n) are two constructors defined. Constructor has the same name as the class and no return value. A class can have multiple constructors. Each time a new object is created, one of the constructors will be invoked.

Aircraft aircraft = new Aircraft("Boeing 727");
or
Aircraft aircraft = new Aircraft();

An instance of the Airplane class can be created using one of the above constructors. Constructors cannot be marked static, final or abstract.

2.1.5

1. private – access only to class
2. protected – access to class and derived classes
3. public – access to all
4. no modifiers – private scope

Which of the above Java access modifier definitions for instance variables or methods are correct?

a. 1, 3, and 4
b. 1, 2, and 3
c. All of the above
d. None of the above

Ans: b

Answer Explanation:

METHODS, CONSTRUCTORS AND ACCESS MODIFIERS

If there is no modifier specified, then the default scope is package scope and the class is visible to all classes in the same package.

Every class, method and instance variable declared has access control whether it's specified or not. For class, only public and default access (no modifier) are valid. Instance variables and methods can be declared as either public, private or protected.

Public methods and instance variables are accessible to the same class and also all other classes. Private members are not accessible to any classes except the same class. Protected members are accessible to the same class and the sub classes.

A protected member can be accessed from a subclass through inheritance even from a different package.

2.1.6

public class Aircraft {

    private String name;

    public String getName() {
        return name;
    }

    public void setName(String name) {
        this.name = name;
    }
}

Why was the member variable name in the above Aircraft class made private with public getter and setter, instead of making it a public variable?

a. Ensures encapsulation
b. Prevents invalid values using checks if needed
c. Provides flexibility, maintainability and extensibility
d. All of the above

Ans: d

Answer Explanation:

Any class that needs to provide access to the member variables as shown above, needs to use the accessor methods. This provides several benefits along with flexibility and maintainability.

Even if the data type of this variable needs to change, still the accessor method will not change. Additional checks or invariants can be added to the accessor methods to ensure data integrity. This provides all the benefits of encapsulation which is also called data hiding.

2.1.7

```
public class Aircraft {

    public Aircraft(String n) {

        this(n, new Date());
    }
    ----
    ----
}
```

In the above code, this(n, new Date()) references

a. Another constructor for the class Aircraft
b. Constructor of super class
c. Method of class Aircraft
d. Method of super class

Ans: a

Answer Explanation:

In a method, this refers to the object on which the method operates.

In a constructor, if the statement has the form this(...), then the constructor calls another constructor of the same class.

public class Aircraft {

METHODS, CONSTRUCTORS AND ACCESS MODIFIERS

```
    String name;
    Date startTime;

    public Aircraft(String n) {

        this(n, new Date());
    }

    public Aircraft(String n , Date d) {
        name = n;
        startTime = d;
    }
}
```

Every constructor has as its first statement, either a call to the overloaded constructor with this(args) or a call to its super class constructor using super().

If either of these are not added explicitly, then the compiler by default adds super(), the default no argument constructor for the super class as the first statement in the constructor.

2.1.8

```
public class Aircraft {
    ----
    public void startEngine() {

        System.out.println("Engine started");
    }

    public void startEngine(long initialRpm) {

        System.out.println("Engine started with initial rpm");
    }
}
```

The above code snippet is an example for

a. overloading

b. overriding
c. abstraction
d. encapsulation

Ans: a

Answer Explanation:

An overloaded method has the same method name and different argument list. Overloaded methods can also change the return type, access modifier and declare new checked exceptions.

The overloaded method should change the method signature which is the argument list, but is not necessary to change return type, access modifier and exception.

A method can be overloaded either in the same class or in the sub class.

2.2 FINAL, FINALIZE AND FINALLY

2.2.1

In Java, constants are denoted by the following keyword:

a. static
b. const
c. abstract
d. final

Ans: d

Answer Explanation:

private static final int *RPM* = 3000;

When a variable is declared as final, the initial value assigned to this variable cannot be changed.

private static final Aircraft aircraft = **new** Aircraft("Boeing 727");

If final is used on an object reference variable as above, the variable aircraft cannot be made to refer to a different object. The data within the object can be changed but the reference variable cannot be made to reference another object.

2.2.2

Since finalize() method is called before garbage collector removes the object, can this method relied for recycling resources that are short in supply?

a. Yes
b. Sometimes
c. Never
d. Always

Ans: c

Answer Explanation:

finalize() method is called just before the garbage collector removes the object. JVM doesn't guarantee that finalizer will be called before object destruction.

An object may wait indefinitely after becoming eligible for garbage collection before its finalize method gets called. For this reason, finalize method cannot be relied for recycling resources.

A dispose method can be created and called manually for releasing resources after usage.

2.2.3

When the final keyword is used

1. In a variable it denotes that the variable is a constant.
2. In a method, represents that the method cannot be overridden by a subclass method.
3. In a class means that the class cannot be sub classed.

Which of the above statements are true?

a. All of the above
b. None of the above
c. 1 and 2
d. 1 and 3

Ans: a

Answer Explanation:

private static final int *MAX_LENGTH* = 20;

When a variable is declared as final, the initial value assigned to this variable cannot be changed.

final keyword on a class means the class cannot be sub classed, which means none of the methods of the class can be overridden. String class of Java library is final.

If a class is not final and if a method needs be prevented from being overridden by the sub classes, the method can be made final.

```java
public class Aircraft {

    private String name;

    public final void fly() {
        System.out.println("Prepare to fly");
    }
}
```

The fly() method is declared final and cannot be overridden by subclasses of the Aircraft class.

2.2.4

```java
public class FinalizerTest1 {

    public static void main(String args[]) {

        System.out.println(FinalizerTest1.test());
    }

    public static int test() {
        try {
            return 0;
        }
        finally {
            System.out.println("Perform clean up");
        }
    }
}
```

```java
public class FinalizerTest2 {

    public static void main(String args[]) {

        System.out.println(FinalizerTest2.test());
    }
```

```java
        public static int test() {

            try {
                throw new Exception();
            }
            catch(Exception e) {
                return 0;
            }
            finally {
                System.out.println("Perform clean up");
            }
        }
}
```

In the above two classes FinalizerTest1 and FinalizerTest2, finally gets called in

a. First
b. Second
c. Both
d. None of the above

Ans: c

Answer Explanation:

When the code throws no exception, try block is executed first followed by finally.

When exception is thrown, all code on try block up to the point where exception is thrown are executed, remaining code in the try block is skipped. Then the matching catch clause is executed, followed by finally.

When exception is thrown that's not caught in the catch clause, code in try block up to the exception is executed, remaining code in try block is skipped, finally clause is executed next, and then the exception is thrown back to the caller of the method.

Similarly return statement in try or catch block is executed after call to finally.

2.3 STATIC FIELDS AND INITIALIZATION BLOCKS

2.3.1

```
public class Aircraft {

    String name;
    Date startTime;

    //initialization block
    {
        startTime = new Date();
    }
    public Aircraft(String n) {
        name = n;
    }
}
```

When an instance of Aircraft is created, when does the initialization block get executed?

a. Never gets executed
b. Before any static methods get executed
c. After the constructor gets executed
d. Before the constructor gets executed

Ans: d

Answer Explanation:

The above sample shows an initialization block which gets executed before the call to constructor when an instance of Aircraft class is created using:

Aircraft a = new Aircraft("Boeing 727");

Instance initialization block gets executed when an instance of a class is created.

2.3.2

```
public class StaticDemo {

    private static final int MAX_SIZE = 10;

    private static int [] numArray = new int [MAX_SIZE];

    static {
        for(int i=0; i< numArray.length; i++) {

            numArray[i] = i+1;
        }
    }
    ----
}
```

Which of the following statement is correct?

Static initialization block gets executed

a. before the constructor gets executed.
b. before any static methods get executed.
c. after the constructor gets executed.
d. when the class is first loaded.

Ans: d

Answer Explanation:

Static initialization block gets executed once, when the class is first loaded. Instance initialization block gets executed when an instance of a class is created, followed by call to the constructor.

The following code sample illustrates the order of execution of initialization blocks.

```
public class InitSample {

    //static initialization block
    static{
        System.out.println("Inside static init block");
    }
```

```java
    //initialization block
    {
        System.out.println("Inside init block");
    }

    public InitSample() {
        System.out.println("Inside constructor");
    }

    public static void main(String [] args) {
        System.out.println("Inside main, creating new instance of InitSample");
        InitSample init = new InitSample();
    }
}
```

Output:

Inside static init block
Inside main, creating new instance of InitSample
Inside init block
Inside constructor

In the above sample, static initialization block is executed when the class is first loaded.

Later inside main(), when a new object init is created, the instance initialization block is executed followed by the constructor.

2.3.3

1. Both static fields and static methods belong to a class and do not operate on any instance of a class.
2. Static initialization blocks can initialize only static variables.
3. Static method cannot be overridden.
4. An instance method can directly access the private static variable of the same class.

Which of the above statements are true?

a. 1, 2, and 4

b. 1, 3, and 4
c. 1, 2, and 3
d. 1, 2, 3, and 4

Ans: d

Answer Explanation:

Static variables and methods belong to the class and exist independent of any instances of the class. All static variables and methods exist before any instance of the class is created. All instances of a class share the same set of static variables.

2.3.4

```
public class InstanceCounter {

    private static int counter = 0;

    public InstanceCounter() {
        counter++;//increment counter
    }

    public static void main(String args[]) {

        InstanceCounter instCounter = null;

        for(int i=0; i<10; i++) {
            instCounter = new InstanceCounter();
        }
        System.out.println("Number of instances: " + counter);

    }
}
```

When the above instanceCounter class is executed, what will be the value of the counter?

a. Won't compile
b. 10
c. 5
d. 0

Ans: b

Answer Explanation:

The static variable counter belongs to the class and does not belong to any instance of the class. It's accessible to all the different instances of the class. In the above sample, inside main(), where 10 new instances are created in the for loop as

```
for(int i=0; i<10; i++) {
    instCounter = new InstanceCounter();
}
```

The constructor gets called every time a new instance is created and the counter value gets incremented to 10.

2.3.5

```
public class StaticDemo {
    public static int factorial(int x) {
        int factx = x;
        while( x > 1) {
            factx = --x * factx;
        }
        return factx;
    }
    public static void main(String [] args) {
        int fact = StaticDemo.factorial(10);
        System.out.println("Factorial of 10 is " + fact);
    }
}
```

What is usually a good criteria to make a method static?
a. If a method is not using any instance variables, that is not modifying the state of the object.
b. Utility methods that work on the instance variables.
c. If the method is modifying the state of the object.
d. If the method is final and cannot be modified.

Ans: a

Answer Explanation:

Usually utility methods that do not access instance variables but work with values of the arguments that are passed to the method are good candidates for static methods.

In the above sample, the method factorial() uses the argument x passed for the computation of factorial value and returns the result.

This method does not access any instance variables and can be used by all instances of the class. This qualifies the factorial() method to be declared as a static method.

Object-Oriented Concepts

3.1 INHERITANCE AND COMPOSITION

3.1.1

```
public class Fish {
    public void swim() { System.out.println("Swimming fish");}
}
public class Shark extends Fish {

}
public static void main(String [] args) {
    Shark s = new Shark();
    s.swim();
}
```

The output for the above program is

a. won't compile
b. run-time exception
c. Swimming fish
d. none of the above

Ans: c

Answer Explanation:

Inheritance relationship is defined by is-a relationship between two classes. In the above sample, Shark is a Fish and Shark is a subtype of Fish, so extends Fish. When a class extends a super class it also inherits all the public and protected member variables and methods from the super class.

The is-a relationship can be implemented using interface inheritance using implements also.

The subclass has the option to override any of the public or protected methods with its own implementation.

3.1.2

public class Fish {

    public void swim() { System.*out*.println("Swimming fish");}
}

public class Shark extends Fish {

    public void swim() { System.*out*.println("Swimming shark");}
}

public static void main(String [] args) {

    Fish f = new Fish();
    Shark s = new Shark();
    f.swim();
    s.swim();
}

Output:

Swimming fish
Swimming shark

The above code snippet is a sample for inheritance and

a. overloading
b. overriding
c. abstraction
d. encapsulation

Ans: b

Answer Explanation:

In the above sample, the method swim() of base class Fish is overridden by the subclass Shark.

The access level of the overriding method can be more restrictive. For example, an inherited protected method cannot be made public but can be made private.

The overriding method cannot throw new or broader exceptions. For example, if the base class method throws EOFException then the overriding method cannot throw any non runtime exceptions other than subclass of EOFException.

final and static methods cannot be overridden.

3.1.3

public class Fish {

    public void swim() { System.*out*.println("Swimming fish");}
}

public class Shark extends Fish {

    public void swim() { System.*out*.println("Swimming shark");}
}

public class TigerShark extends Shark {

    public void swim() { System.*out*.println("Swimming tiger shark");
}
}

public static void main(String [] args) {

    Fish f = new TigerShark();
    f.swim();
}

Output:

Swimming tiger shark

The above code snippet is a sample for inheritance and

a. overloading
b. abstraction
c. polymorphism
d. encapsulation

Ans: c

Answer Explanation:

Any java object that passes more than one is-a relationship can be considered polymorphic. In the above sample TigerShark is a Shark and TigerShark is also a Fish.

Polymorphism enables the overridden instance methods to be dynamically invoked based on the objects type.

In the above sample, the overridden method swim() of TigerShark class is invoked correctly at runtime, even though at compile time it is referring to the swim() method of the base class Fish.

3.1.4

Polymorphism is the phenomenon by which the object knows which method to invoke depending on its position in the inheritance hierarchy.

The above statement is

a. True
b. False

Ans: a

Answer Explanation:

Polymorphism is the phenomenon by which an object knows which method to invoke depending on its position in the inheritance hierarchy, this is possible due to late binding or dynamic binding where the method to be called is determined at runtime depending on the object's type.

3.1.5

Super class for all classes in Java is

a. Class
b. Object
c. String
d. Thread

Ans: b

Answer Explanation:

Object is the super class for all objects on java. All objects are direct or indirect descendents of the Object class and as a result, all objects inherit the methods of the Object class.

Some of the commonly used inherited methods of the Object class are hashCode(), equals(), clone(), toString(), finalize(), and wait().

3.1.6

public class JumboJet extends Aircraft {

    public JumboJet(String name, Date date) {

        super(name, date);
    }

    public void startEngine() {
        ----
        super.startEngine();
    }

}

In the above code snippet, super(name, date) and super.startEngine() refers to:

a. constructor and method in the same class
b. constructor and method in the super class
c. the reference is incorrect.
d. none of the above

Ans: b

Answer Explanation:

Every constructor has as its first statement, either a call to the overloaded constructor with this(args) or a call to its super class constructor using super().

If either of these are not added explicitly, then the compiler by default adds super(), the default no argument constructor for the super class as the first statement in the constructor.

3.1.7

```java
public class Fish {
    public void swim() { System.out.println("Swimming fish");}
}
public class Shark extends Fish {
    public void swim() { System.out.println("Swimming shark");}
}
public class TigerShark extends Shark {
    public void swim() {System.out.println("Swimming tiger shark");}
}
public static void main(String [] args) {
    Fish f = new TigerShark();
}
```

In the above sample, when the constructor of the TigerShark class is invoked using

Fish f = new TigerShark();

What other constructors are invoked?

a. Fish
b. Fish and Object
c. Shark and Fish
d. Shark, Fish and Object

Ans: d

Answer Explanation:

Every constructor invokes the constructor of its super class with implicit call to super(). In the above sample, TigerShark constructor is invoked first, which invokes the Shark constructor, which invokes the Fish constructor, which invokes the Object constructor.

The Object constructor completes, followed by completion of Fish, Shark and TigerShark constructors.

3.1.8

```
public class Train {

    Engine engine;
    Carriage carriage;
    Wagon wagon;

    public void startTrain() {

        engine.startEngine();
        carriage.closeDoors();
        wagon.connectWagon();
    }
}
```

The above sample is an example for

a. inheritance
b. abstraction
c. composition
d. polymorphism

Ans: c

Answer Explanation:

The above sample is an example for composition also referred as composite pattern. When the relationship between two classes is a has-a relationship, then composition is used.

The code can be reused as needed from the contained classes Engine, Carriage and Wagon. Also, the visibility can be controlled by the container class Train.

The startTrain() method in the above sample, calls methods of three other classes, this is called forwarding and is similar to the wrapper class of Decorator pattern.

3.1.9

What's a good criteria to use Inheritance vs Composition while designing?

a. Always use inheritance
b. Always use composition
c. Inheritance for is-a relationships
d. None of the above

Ans: c

Answer Explanation:

In inheritance, subclasses depend on the super class and any implementation changes to the super class can break the subclass. Composition also provides all the inheritance functionalities with more flexibility by calling the methods of the contained classes.

Composition can be used when has-a relationship is needed and also can be used to overcome some of the issues with inheritance as mentioned above. If there is a is-a relationship, inheritance can be used. If code reuse and polymorphism is needed, and is-a relationship doesn't exist, then composition can be used.

3.1.10

A class can be prevented from being subclassed by making it final. Another way to prevent subclassing a class is to

a. Make all methods final.
b. Make the constructor private.
c. Make all member variables final.
d. Make all methods private.

Ans: b

Answer Explanation:

A class can be prevented from being inherited by making the class final or by making the constructor private.

When the constructor of a class is made private, it cannot be inherited or subclassed. The subclass constructor will invoke the superclass constructor during object creation which will not be possible due to a private super class constructor. When constructor is private, the class cannot be instantiated or subclassed.

3.2 ABSTRACT CLASS AND INTERFACE

3.2.1

public abstract class Tree {

    public void absorbNutrients() {

        System.*out*.println("Absorbing nutrients");
    }
    public abstract void makeFruit();
}

public class PeachTree extends Tree {

    public void makeFruit() {

        System.*out*.println("Make peach fruit");
    }
}

1. Abstract class factors out common behavior of classes to a higher level.
2. Abstract class has at least one abstract method.
3. An abstract class is same as an interface.

Which of the above statements are true?

a. 1, 2, and 3
b. 1 and 3
c. 2 and 3
d. 1 and 2

Ans: d

Answer Explanation:

An abstract class usually has at least one abstract method. An abstract class is different from an interface since abstract class can have one or more methods implemented while an interface cannot have any implemented methods.

An abstract class cannot be instantiated, only a sub class of an abstract class can be instantiated. An abstract class cannot be made final or static.

An abstract method cannot be private as private methods cannot be overridden.

3.2.2

If there are no abstract methods in a class, is it possible to make the class abstract?

a. Yes
b. No
c. If some of the methods are implemented
d. None of the above

Ans: a

Answer Explanation:

A class with no abstract method can be made an abstract class. This is done sometimes to prevent the class from being instantiated. Only a subclass of this class can be instantiated.

If at least one method in a class is declared abstract, the class has to be declared abstract to avoid a compiler error.

3.2.3

```
public interface Reptile {
     void move();
}
```

```
public class Turtle implements Reptile {

     public void move() {
          System.out.println("Swim in water");
```

            }
}

public class Lizard implements Reptile {

    public void move() {
        System.*out*.println("Walk on land");
    }
}

Which of the below statement regarding interfaces is false?

a. Interfaces in Java, recover much of the functionalities of multiple inheritance.
b. An interface can extend another interface.
c. Instant fields and static methods cannot be used in interfaces as interfaces cannot be initiated.
d. Constants cannot be used in interfaces.

Ans: d

Answer Explanation:

The interface inheritance defines is-a relationship between two classes. An interface declares all the methods with no implementation. The interface gives details on what the class can do without details on how to do. An interface can extend one or more interfaces.

public interface Animal {
    void move();
}

public interface Reptile extends Animal {
    void move();
}

Typing public for interface methods are redundant, as the interfaces methods are implicitly public and abstract. Also all variables defined in an interface are implicitly public, static and final.

Since an interface method is abstract, it cannot be made final.

3.2.4

public interface Propeller {

    int rpm = 3000;
    void startPropeller();
}

In the above declaration, the variable rpm is implicitly

a. public
b. static
c. final
d. all of the above

Ans: d

Answer Explanation:

All variables defined in an interface are implicitly public, static and final. All interfaces methods are also implicitly public.

Interface can declare static final variables, but not instance variables. Instance variables are not allowed, as an interface cannot be instantiated.

3.2.5

Difference between abstract class and interface:

1. All methods of an interface need to be implemented by the sub class, while only the abstract methods of an abstract class need to be implemented by the subclass.
2. Some methods can be fully implemented in an abstract class but not in an interface.
3. Abstract class can be final but interface cannot be final.
4. Abstract class can be initiated but interface cannot be initiated.

Which of the above statements are true?

a. 1 and 2

b. 1, 2, and 3
c. 1, 2, and 4
d. 1, 2, 3, and 4

Ans: a

Answer Explanation:

Both abstract class and interface cannot be final. Also, abstract classes as well as interfaces cannot be initiated.

3.2.6

Which of the following is not valid to be used with an instanceof expression for an Object?

a. transient
b. interface
c. class
d. abstract class

Ans: a

Answer Explanation:

instanceof operator can be used to find if an object is of a specific type.

Aircraft aircraft = **new** Aircraft("Boeing 727");

if(aircraft **instanceof** Aircraft) {
    System.*out*.println("aircraft is an instanceof AbstractAircraft");
}

Output:

aircraft is an instanceof AbstractAircraft

instanceof operator can be used with an interface, class or an abstract class.

3.2.7

An interface is more flexible than an abstract class because

a. Interface does not provide any method implementation.
b. Interface is more light weight than abstract class.
c. A class can implement any number of interfaces but can extend only one Abstract class.
d. Abstract class cannot be final.

Ans: c

Answer Explanation:

Java does not support multiple inheritance, so a class can extend only one super class. If a class is already extending a class, it cannot extend an abstract class also. But the class can implement any number of interfaces. This makes using interfaces more flexible than using abstract classes.

Abstract classes are usually used when there is some generic functionalities that are common to all subclasses and also there is a is-a relationship. Template method design pattern is a good example for using abstract classes where some common functionalities are provided in some methods along with other abstract methods.

```
public abstract class VeggieWrap {

    public final void prepare() {
        addVeggies();
        addCheese();
        wrap();
    }

    protected abstract void addVeggies();
    protected abstract void addCheese();
    public void wrap() {System.out.println("Wrapping");}
}
```

The strengths of interface and abstract classes can be combined by defining an interface and then providing a skeletal implementation of the interface using an AbstractInterface class.

Examples for AbstractInterface classes are AbstractCollection, AbstractSet, AbstractList etc.

3.2.8

Considerations while designing a class:

a. Choose inheritance or composition depending on the relationship between classes
b. Favor immutability to simplify access and functionalities.
c. Prefer interfaces to abstract classes
d. All of the above

Ans: d

Answer Explanation:

Composition can be chosen over inheritance if there is no is-a relationship between subclass and the superclass.

A class can be made immutable by

1. Making the fields private and final.
2. Making the methods final so they cannot be overridden.
3. Not providing mutator methods for modifying the fields.

Immutable objects are thread safe and are easy to develop and test. Implementing an interface allows flexibility because when a class extends an abstract class it cannot subclass any other class.

3.3 CLONEABLE INTERFACE

3.3.1

1. Clone method is used to make bit-wise copy of an object.
2. Clone method is a protected method of the Object class.
3. If an object has reference to another object, then the cloned and the original object will be referencing the same object.
4. If data fields in the object are basic types like integer, then bitwise operation of clone method works fine.

Which of the above statements are true?

a. 1, 2, and 3
b. 1, 2, and 4
c. 1, 2, 3, and 4
d. None of the above

Ans: c

Answer Explanation:

To support cloning, the class needs to implement the Cloneable interface and define the clone() method. The clone() method is defined in the Object class and not in the Cloneable interface.

The clone() method of the Object class which provides the default clone functionality, makes a bit-wise copy of the object which is a shallow copy. This works fine if all the fields are of basic type like integer.

public class Aircraft **implements** Cloneable {

    protected Object clone() **throws** CloneNotSupportedException {

    }
}

If a field has an object reference, then shallow copy will not be enough, because the cloned object will also be pointing to the same object reference.

In this scenario, the default clone functionality will not be sufficient and the clone() method should be implemented to make a deep copy.

3.3.2

```
//current date and time
Date startDate = new Date();
Date aDate = startDate;
int delayedHours = 4;

//for delayed time
long startTimeInMillisecond = startDate.getTime();
long delayInMillisecond = delayedHours * 60 * 60 * 1000L;

//change startTime
startDate.setTime(startTimeInMillisecond + delayInMillisecond);
```

In the above code, both startDate and aDate are referring to the same object and the time change to startDate is also applied to aDate.

Which of the following initiation can be used to copy the state of startDate object to aDate so that both objects function independently?

1. Date aDate = new Date(startDate.getTime());
2. Date aDate = (Date) startDate.clone();
3. Date aDate = new Date();

a. 1 and 2
b. 1 and 3
c. 2 and 3
d. 1, 2, and 3

Ans: a

Answer Explanation:

The clone of an object has a bit wise copy of the object. To support cloning, the class needs to implement the Cloneable interface and define the clone() method. The clone() method is defined in the Object class and not in the Cloneable interface.

CLONEABLE INTERFACE

```
public class Aircraft implements Cloneable {
    ----
    protected Object clone() throws CloneNotSupportedException {
        ----
    }
}
```

Invoking the clone() method on an instance that doesn't implement the Cloneable interface throws CloneNotSupportedException.

3.3.3

```
public class Aircraft implements Cloneable {

    String name;
    Date startTime;
    ----
    protected Object clone() throws CloneNotSupportedException {

        Aircraft a = (Aircraft) super.clone();
        a.startTime = (Date) startTime.clone();
        return a;
    }
}
```

In the above code, inside the clone() method, startTime.clone() is called so that
a. startTime of the cloned object is not a copy of the original object.
b. startTime of the cloned object is not referencing the startTime of the original Object.
c. startTime of the cloned object is referencing the startTime of the original Object.
d. None of the above.

Ans: b

Answer Explanation:

The cloned object is a bit-wise copy of the original object. If the data fields in the cloned object are basic types like integer, then bitwise copy works fine.

But if the field is a reference to another object like the Date object in the above sample, then the cloned object will also be referencing the same object.

In this scenario, the default bit wise copy functionality provided by the clone() method of Object class is not enough and the clone() method needs to be implemented by cloning the object reference.

a.startTime = (Date) startTime.clone();

The above line in the clone() method ensures that the startTime Date object is a separate copy and not referencing the original Date object.

3.4 INNER CLASSES

3.4.1

1. An object of the inner class can access private members of the outer class.
2. Inner classes can be hidden from the other classes in the same package.
3. Inner classes are phenomenon of the compiler and not of the virtual machine.
4. Static inner class does not have access to private members of the outer class.

Which of the above statements are true?

a. 1, 2, and 3
b. 1, 2, and 4
c. 1, 3, and 4
d. 1, 2, 3, and 4

Ans: d

Answer Explanation:

An inner class is a class that is defined inside another class. Inner classes can be hidden from the other classes and inner class can access private members of the outer class that created it.

public class Aircraft {

    private int modelNumber;
    ----
    private class AircraftCapacity {

    }
}

AircraftCapacity is a private class inside the Aircraft class. This way, only methods of the Aircraft class can create object of AircraftCapacity class.

Inner classes can be used when the outer class needs helper objects that may need access to the private members of the outer class. In this sample, AircraftCapacity will need access to the private member variable modelNumber of Aircraft class to calculate the capacity.

3.4.2

public class LinkedListDemo {

    Node head;
    Node tail;

    private static class Node {

    }

}

Static inner class is used when

a. the inner class needs to access variables in the outer class.
b. the inner class does not need to access variables in the outer class.
c. the inner class has static variables or methods.
d. the outer class has static variables or methods.

Ans: b

Answer Explanation:

If the inner class is used to just hide one class inside another and reference to the outer object is not needed, then the inner class can be made static.

A static inner class can access only static members of the outer class. An inner class can access static and non static members of the outer class.

In the above sample, the inner class Node is static as it does not reference any fields of the outer class. Inner class Node is declared private to be hidden from the other classes in the package.

INNER CLASSES

3.4.3

```
public class AircraftSet extends AbstractSet {
    ----
    public Iterator iterator() {
        return new AircraftIterator();
    }

    private class AircraftIterator implements Iterator {
        ----
    }
}
```

In the above code snippet,

a. Each instance of inner class AircraftIterator is associated with instance of the containing class AircraftSet.
b. Each instance of inner class AircraftIterator is not associated with instance of the containing class AircraftSet.
c. AircraftIterator is an anonymous inner class.
d. None of the above.

Ans: a

Answer Explanation:

An instance of the inner class cannot be created without the instance of the outer class. An inner class can access static and non static members of the outer class.

In the above sample, AircraftIterator is a private inner class of AircraftSet class, so only methods of the AircraftSet class can create an instance of AircraftIterator.

3.4.4

public static void sortAircraftAnonymous(List<Aircraft> aircraft) {

    Collections.*sort*(aircraft, new Comparator<Aircraft>() {
      @Override
    public int compare(Aircraft x, Aircraft y) {

```
                int difference =
                    x.getModelNumber() - y.getModelNumber();

                if (difference < 0) return -1;
                if (difference > 0) return 1;
                return 0;
            }
        });
    }
```

In the above code snippet, new Comparator() represents

a. Inner class
b. Anonymous inner class
c. Static member class
d. Abstract class

Ans: b

Answer Explanation:

In the above sample, the second argument of the method Collections.sort is a Comparator instance. Since only a single object of the Comparator interface is needed, a new instance can be created without a name. Since there is no name for this instance of the inner class, it's called an anonymous inner class.

Any class that implements the Comparator interface should define the compare() method for sorting. The above syntax looks a bit complicated but it's same as creating and referencing a new inner class which implements the Comparator interface. The advantage of using anonymous inner class is compactness of the code.

The same method can be implemented using the inner class as below:

```
public static void sortAircraft(List<Aircraft> aircraft) {

    class AircraftComparator implements Comparator<Aircraft> {

        @Override
        public int compare(Aircraft x, Aircraft y) {

            int difference =
                x.getModelNumber() - y.getModelNumber();
```

```java
                if (difference < 0) return -1;
                if (difference > 0) return 1;
                return 0;
            }
        }
        Collections.sort(aircraft, new AircraftComparator());
    }
    public static void main(String [] args) {

        Aircraft a = new Aircraft("Boeing 757");
        a.setModelNumber(200);
        Aircraft b = new Aircraft("Boeing 747");
        b.setModelNumber(150);
        Aircraft c = new Aircraft("Boeing 737");
        c.setModelNumber(100);

        List<Aircraft> aircraftList = new ArrayList<Aircraft>();
        aircraftList.add(a);
        aircraftList.add(b);
        aircraftList.add(c);

        AnonymousDemo.sortAircraft(aircraftList);

        for(Aircraft x : aircraftList) {

            System.out.println("modelNumber: " + x.getModelNumber());
        }
    }
}
```

Output:

modelNumber: 100
modelNumber: 150
modelNumber: 200

3.5 RUNTIME TYPE IDENTIFICATION

3.5.1

```java
import java.lang.reflect.Field;
import java.lang.reflect.Method;
import java.lang.reflect.Constructor;

public static void getClassDetails() throws Exception{
    try {
        String className = "Aircraft";
        Class cl = Class.forName(className);

        //print field names
        Field[] fields = cl.getDeclaredFields();
        for(int i= 0; i < fields.length; i++) {
            System.out.println("field Name: " +
            fields[i].getName());
        }

        System.out.println("\n");
        //print method names
        Method[] methods = cl.getDeclaredMethods();
        for(int i= 0; i < methods.length; i++) {
            System.out.println("method Name: " +
            methods[i].getName());
        }

        System.out.println("\n");
        //print constructor names
        Constructor[] constructors = cl.getDeclaredConstructors();
        for(int i= 0; i < constructors.length; i++) {
            System.out.println("constructor Name: " +
            constructors[i].getName());
        }
    }
    catch(Exception e) {
        throw e;
    }
}
```

RUNTIME TYPE IDENTIFICATION

In the above getClassDetails() method, the class details are obtained using:

1. Type-casting
2. Run-Time Type Identification
3. Reflection
4. Generics

a. 1 and 2
b. 1 and 3
c. 2 and 3
d. 3 and 4

Ans: c

Answer Explanation:

Java runtime maintains runtime type identification (RTTI) on all objects for keeping track of class of an object, for executing methods etc. An instance of the class Class can be obtained using

Class cl = Class.*forName*(className);

Class instance cl can be used for getting the fields, methods and constructor of the class as given in the sample above. The reflection mechanism used for analyzing the capabilities of a class is provided by java.lang.reflect package. Output for the above program is given below.

Output:

field Name: name
field Name: startTime
field Name: modelNumber

method Name: main
method Name: equals
method Name: toString
method Name: hashCode
method Name: clone
method Name: compareTo
method Name: getName
method Name: setName
method Name: getModelNumber

method Name: setModelNumber
method Name: startEngine
method Name: startEngine
method Name: stopEngine
method Name: setAircraftStartTime

constructor Name: Aircraft
constructor Name: Aircraft

The two startEngine are overloaded methods and the two Aircraft are overloaded constructors.

Exceptions, Input Streams and Serialization

4.1 EXCEPTION HIERARCHY

4.1.1

The base class for all exceptions is

a. Exception
b. RunTimeException
c. Error
d. Throwable

Ans: d

Answer Explanation:

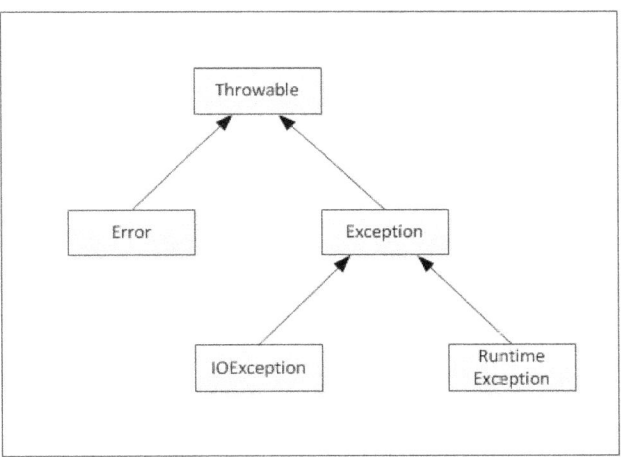

All exceptions descend from class Throwable.

4.1.2

The base class for classes Error and Exception is

a. Exception

b. RunTimeException
c. Error
d. Throwable

Ans: d

Answer Explanation:

Throwable is the base class for Error and Exception.

4.1.3

The base class for classes IOException and RuntimeException is

a. Exception
b. RunTimeException
c. Error
d. Throwable

Ans: a

Answer Explanation:

Exception is the base class for IOException and RuntimeException

4.2 ERROR AND RUNTIME EXCEPTION

4.2.1

Which of the following describe the class Error?

1. Thrown due to internal error and resource exhaustion in java runtime system
2. Happens rarely
3. Should not be thrown by user
4. Program should notify user and exit gracefully

a. 1, 3, and 4
b. 1, 2, and 4
c. 2, 3, and 4
d. 1, 2, 3, and 4

Ans: d

Answer Explanation:

Errors are generated by java runtime and represents internal errors like out of memory. Errors occur rarely and are beyond the control of the user. The program should handle errors gracefully by notifying the users before exiting.

4.2.2

Exceptions that are subclass of RuntimeException have the following problems

a. Unsupported operation
b. Out of bounds array access
c. Null pointer access
d. All of the above

Ans: d

Answer Explanation:

```
public static void main(String [] args) {

    try {
        int [] a = new int[1];

        a[0] = 1;
        a[1] = 2;
    }
    catch(RuntimeException e) {
        e.printStackTrace();
    }
}
```

The above program throws java.lang.ArrayIndexOutOfBoundsException.

ArrayIndexOutOfBoundsException is a subclass of RuntimeException which is happening because of programming error. When a[1] is accessed, it is not available since the size of the array is 1.

This RuntimeException has happened because of programming error and should be fixed. This exception need not be caught in the catch block and is called unchecked exception.

4.2.3

Exceptions that are not subclass of RuntimeException have the following problems

a. FileNotFoundException
b. MalformedURLException
c. ClassNotFoundException
d. All of the above

Ans: d

Answer Explanation:

The above exceptions that do not inherit RuntimeException are called checked exceptions and they should be handled by the user or should be propagated by rethrowing the exceptions.

```java
public static void readAndWrite() {

    BufferedReader in = null;
    PrintWriter out = null;

    try {
        in = new BufferedReader(new FileReader("InputAircraft.txt"));

        out = new PrintWriter(new FileWriter("OutputAircraft.txt"));

        String str;
        while ((str = in.readLine()) != null) {

            out.println(str);
        }
    }
    catch(IOException e) {
        e.printStackTrace();
    }
    finally {
        in.close();
        out.close();
    }
}
```

In the above sample, IOException which is a checked exception is caught and handled. This exception can be propagated to the caller as

```java
public static void readAndWrite() throws IOException{
    ...

    try {
        ...
    }
    catch(IOException e) {
        throw e;
    }

    ...
}
```

4.2.4

1. Any exception that is subclassed from class Error or class RuntimeException is called unchecked exception.
2. All exceptions other than ones subclassed from Error or RuntimeException are called checked exceptions.
3. Checked exceptions should be handled and propagated by the user.
4. Error is beyond user's control and RuntimeException is caused by programming error.

Which of the above statements are true?

a. 1, 3, and 4
b. 1, 2, and 4
c. 2, 3, and 4
d. 1, 2, 3, and 4

Ans: d

Answer Explanation:

RuntimeException happens because of programming error, Error because of internal error like resource exhaustion that is not in the control of the user.

Exceptions that are subclass of RuntimeException and Error are unchecked exceptions. All other exceptions that are not subclass of RuntimeException and Error are checked exceptions.

4.3 TRY AND CATCH

4.3.1

```
public Connection getConnection() throws NamingException,
                                          SQLException
{
    Connection conn = null;
    try {
        Context jndiContext = new InitialContext();

        DataSource dataSource =
             (DataSource) jndiContext.lookup("test");

        conn = dataSource.getConnection();
    }
    catch(NamingException e) {
        throw e;
    }
    catch(SQLException e) {
        throw e;
    }
    return conn;
}
```

In the above code snippet, the exception is rethrown to the caller and is

a. suppressed
b. propagated
c. redefined
d. All of the above

Ans: b

Answer Explanation:

In the above sample, both NamingException and SQLException are caught and rethrown to the caller. Since these exceptions are propagated to the caller, they are advertised in the method as

public Connection getConnection() throws NamingException,
                                         SQLException

These exceptions should be caught and handled by the caller of this method.

```
public void handleConnection() throws SQLException {

    Connection conn = null;

    try {
        conn = getConnection();
    }
    catch(NamingException e) {
        e.printStackTrace();
    }
    catch(SQLException e) {
        throw e;
    }
    finally {
        conn.close();
    }
}
```

NamingException and SQLException are caught and handled. Also in the finally block, connection is closed using conn.close().

The finally block is always called regardless if

- the try block is executed fully
- an exception is thrown that is handled or rethrown
- an exception is thrown and is not caught.

Any code that handles cleaning and recycling of resources should be handled in the finally block.

4.3.2

IOException is the base class of FileNotFoundException.

If both these exceptions need to be caught in a catch block, which one should be caught first?

a. FileNotFoundException followed by IOException

b. IOException followed by FileNotFoundException
c. FileNotFoundException followed by Exception
d. IOException followed by Exception

Ans: a

Answer Explanation:

FileNotFoundException should be caught first as this is a subclass of IOException. If IOException was caught first, then every time when FileNotFoundException is thrown, the catch block for IOException will be executed.

```
public static void readAndWrite() {

    BufferedReader in = null;
    PrintWriter out = null;

    try {
        in = new BufferedReader(new FileReader("InputAircraft.txt"));

        out = new PrintWriter(new FileWriter("OutputAircraft.txt"));

        String str;
        while ((str = in.readLine()) != null) {

            out.println(str);
        }
    }
    catch(FileNotFoundException fe) {
        fe.printStackTrace();
    }
    catch(IOException e) {
        e.printStackTrace();
    }
    finally {
        in.close();
        out.close();
    }
}
```

4.3.3

finally gets called when

a. try block gets fully executed
b. exception is caught and then handled or rethrown
c. exception is not caught
d. all of the above

Ans: d

Answer Explanation

```
public void handleConnection() throws SQLException {

    Connection conn = null;

    try {
         conn = getConnection();
    }
    catch(NamingException e) {
         e.printStackTrace();
    }
    catch(SQLException e) {
         throw e;
    }
    finally {
         conn.close();
    }
}
```

In the above sample, finally block in which the connection is closed is always executed in each the following scenarios.

1. When the try block is executed and no exception is thrown.
2. When NamingException is thrown and handled.
3. When SQLException is thrown and propagated.
4. If the code throws an exception that is not caught in the catch blocks, and as a result gets rethrown to the caller.

4.4 FILE INPUT AND OUTPUT STREAMS

4.4.1

```
public static void readAndWrite() {

    BufferedReader in = null;
    PrintWriter out = null;

    try {
        in = new BufferedReader(
            new FileReader("InputAircraftDetails.txt"));

        out = new PrintWriter(
            new FileWriter("OutputAircraftDetails.txt"));

        String str;
        while ((str = in.readLine()) != null) {

            out.println(str);
        }
    }
    catch(IOException e) {
        e.printStackTrace();
    }
    finally {
        in.close();
        out.close();
    }
}
```

In the above code snippet, will the lines from the source text file copied to the destination text file?

a. no
b. yes

Ans: b

Answer Explanation:

While reading from or writing to files, Java uses a set of stream filters for converting between unicode encoded text used by java and character encoding used by the local operating system. All these classes descend from abstract classes Reader and Writer.

FileReader used in the above sample is a subclass of InputStreamReader which is a subclass of abstract class Reader. Similarly, FileWriter is a subclass of OutputStreamWriter which is a subclass of Writer.

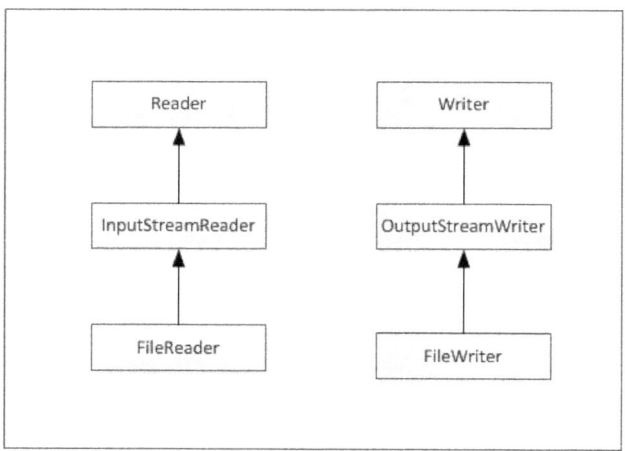

For reading the text, readLine() method of BufferedReader is used. BufferedReader takes the InputStreamReader as constructor that converts bytes to Unicode. PrintWriter constructor takes an OutputStreamWriter to convert Unicode characters to bytes.

in = new BufferedReader(new FileReader("InputAircraftDetails.txt"));

out = new PrintWriter(new FileWriter("OutputAircraftDetails.txt"));

PrintWriter prints characters in text format using out.println();

4.5 OBJECT SERIALIZATION

4.5.1

public class Customer implements Serializable {

    private static final long *serialVersionUID* = 8447024394585228398L;

    private String firstName;
    private String lastName;
    private int age;
}

Which of the following statements are true regarding Serializable interface?

a. Provides automatic serialization for translating the object state to a format that can be stored in a file, memory or transmitted across network and recovered later.
b. All subclasses of Serializable class are also Serializable.
c. The Serializable interface has no methods or fields.
d. All of the above

Ans: d

Answer Explanation:

In Java, object serialization is the process of converting objects into binary format to be stored in a disk or to be transmitted in the network. Deserialization is the reverse process of converting the binary format to object.

The Serializable interface has no methods or fields and serves as a semantic to indicate that the object is serialized.

The subclass of a class that implements Serializable is also Serializable, provided the superclass provides a no argument constructor. The no argument constructor is needed to initialize the state of the superclass.

4.5.2

To allow the subclass to be serialized, a non-serializable superclass needs to provide

a. a no-argument constructor that is public
b. fields that are initialized
c. public, protected or package fields
d. all of the above

Ans: a

Answer Explanation:

When the superclass is non-serializable and the subclass needs to be serialized, the subclass will have to save and restore the state of superclasses public, protected or packaged fields. For this, the superclass should provide an accessible no-argument constructor to initialize the classes state.

A subclass implementing Serializable when the no-argument accessible constructor is not provided by the superclass, will result in a runtime error.

4.5.3

public class Customer implements Serializable {

    private static final long *serialVersionUID =*
    8447024394585228398L;

    private String firstName;
    private String lastName;
    private int age;
}

In the above code snippet, what is serialVersionUID used for?

a. Provides versioning for the serialized data.
b. serialVersionUID is stored during serialization.

c. During deserialization, serialVersionUID is extracted and compared with the loaded class.
d. All of the above

Ans: d

Answer Explanation:

In Java, object serialization is the process of converting objects into binary format to be stored in a disk or to be transmitted in the network. Deserialization is the reverse process of converting the binary format to object.

When the object is serialized, serialVersionUID is serialized along with the other contents. During deserialization, the serialVersionUID is extracted and compared with that of the class. If the serialVersionUIDs don't match, InvalidClassException is thrown.

This is done to prevent issues due to deserialising data that was created using a previous version of the class into the newer version of the class.

4.5.4

public class Customer implements Serializable {

    private String firstName;
    private String lastName;
    private int age;
}

The above Customer class implements Serializable, but does not define a serialVersionUID variable with a value. If the Customer object is stored to persistence, and later this serialized object is deserialized using a modified version of Customer object,

a. the object gets deserialized
b. it throws InvalidClassException
c. object doesn't get deserialized properly
d. None of the above

Ans: b

Answer Explanation:

In the Customer class, since serialVersionUID was not defined, serialVersionUID is generated based on the fields, methods, class name etc.

When the class is modified, the serialVersionUID generated for the new class doesn't match with the one stored with the old serialized object, InvalidClassException is thrown.

If serialVersionUID is specified in the file as

private static final long *serialVersionUID* = 8447024394585228398L;

Even if the class changes, as long as the serialVersionUID remains unchanged, deserialization from the data stored using older version of the class is possible. If a new field address is added that doesn't have data stored, it will be set to null. If there are stored data for fields that are not present in the newer class, they will be ignored.

SerialVersionUID can be generated from command-line using

serialver Customer

where Customer is the class name.

4.5.5

public class Customer **implements** Serializable {

    private static final long *serialVersionUID*
    = 8447024394585228398L;

    private String firstName;
    private String lastName;
    private int age;
    private transient int ssn;

    public Customer(String fn, String ln, int a, int s) {

```java
            this.firstName = fn;
            this.lastName = ln;
            this.age = a;
            this.ssn = s;
    }

    public String getFirstName() { return firstName; }
    public void setFirstName(String firstName) { this.firstName = firstName; }
    public String getLastName() { return lastName; }
    public void setLastName(String lastName) { this.lastName = lastName; }
    public int getAge() { return age; }
    public void setAge(int age) { this.age = age; }
    public int getSsn() { return ssn; }
    public void setSsn(int ssn) { this.ssn = ssn; }

    public String toString() {

            final StringBuilder sb = new StringBuilder();
            sb.append(this.getClass().getSimpleName());
            sb.append("firstName=").append(firstName);
            sb.append(", lastName=").append(lastName);
            sb.append(", age=").append(age);
            sb.append(", ssn=").append(ssn);
            return sb.toString();
    }
}

public class SerializableDemo {

    public static void serialize() {
        try {
            Customer cust =
                new Customer("Huck", "Finn", 12, 111222333);

            FileOutputStream fo =
                new FileOutputStream("customerData.ser");

            ObjectOutputStream os = new ObjectOutputStream(fo);
            os.writeObject(cust);
            os.close();
        }
```

```java
            catch(Exception e) {
                e.printStackTrace();
            }
        }

    public static void deserialize() {

        try {
            FileInputStream fi = new
            FileInputStream("customerData.ser");

            ObjectInputStream is = new ObjectInputStream(fi);

            Customer customer = (Customer) is.readObject();
            is.close();

            System.out.println(customer.toString());

            //cleanup file created
            new File("customerData.ser").delete();
        }
        catch(Exception e) {
            e.printStackTrace();
        }
    }

    public static void main(String [] args) {

        SerializableDemo.serialize();
        SerializableDemo.deserialize();
    }
}
```

When SerializableDemo is run, what will be the value of ssn in the output?

a. 111222333
b. 0
c. 111
d. 111222

Ans: b

Answer Explanation:

Since ssn is declared as transient, ssn value will not be serialized. Transient keyword is used to prevent serialization.

In Java, Object serialization is the process of converting objects into binary format to be stored in a disk or to be transmitted in the network. Deserialization is the reverse process of converting the binary format to object.

4.5.6

To prevent serialization, a variable can be declared

a. transient
b. static
c. transient or static
d. volatile

Ans: c

Answer Explanation:

If any field is declared transient or static it will not be part of the object's state and will not be part of the serialization process.

4.5.7

What are the methods that can be used to override the default Serialization process?

a. serialize() and deserialize()
b. writeObject() and readObject()
c. writeExternal() and readExternal()
d. All of the above

Ans: b

Answer Explantion:

If writeObject() and readObject() methods are defined in the class, then these methods will be invoked instead of default serialization. Serialization and deserialization can be customized by overriding these two methods.

4.5.8

Difference between Serializable and Externalizable: which of the following are true?

a. Serializable is a marker interface with no method, while Externalizable has writeExternal() and readExternal() methods.
b. When a class is Serialized it takes care of the Serialization process, while for Externalizable interface it's the users responsibility to implement the serialization process.
c. With serialization, performance cannot be improved except by making the fields transient or static so that they are not serialized. With Externalizable, since custom implementation has to be made, performance can be improved.
d. All of the above

Ans: d

Answer Explanation:

Externalizable provides writeExternal() and readExternal() methods that gives flexibility over the serialization process for improving performance, while Serializable relies on the default serialization provided by Java.

Language Features

5.1 GENERICS

5.1.1

```
//using Generics
List<String> gl = new ArrayList<String>();
gl.add("a");
String value = gl.get(0);
System.out.println("ArrayList gl value : " + value);

//not using Generics
List al = new ArrayList();
al.add("a");
al.add(1);

value = (String) al.get(0);
System.out.println("ArrayList al first value: " + value);
value = (String) al.get(1);// throws ClassCastException
System.out.println("ArrayList al second value: " + value);
```

In the above code, Generics add stability to the code by making bugs detectable at

a. compile time
b. run time
c. all of the above
d. none of the above

Ans: a

Answer Explanation:

Generics feature was added in Java 5 to add compile time type checking and for removing the occurrence of ClassCastException. In the above example, Generics in List gl spares casting, as the compiler performs type checking and casting.

List al does not use Generics and the programmer has to keep track of object types and casting. Running the above code throws ClassCastException, as al.get(1) has been cast to the wrong type which is detected only at runtime.

5.1.2

class1:

```
public class Spacecraft {

    private Object object;
    public void set( Object object) { this.object = object; }
    public Object get() {return object;}
}
```

class2:

```
public class Spacecraft<T> {

    private T t;
    public void set(T t) { this.t = t; }
    public T get() {return t;}
}
```

In the above code, class2 uses Generics while class1 does not. Setting and getting two different objects in class2 will result in a compile time error, but in class1 will result in a

a. compile time error
b. run time error
c. no error
d. none of the above

Ans: b

Answer Explanation:

In class1, the set() and get() methods take and return an Object instance. If a String object is set in the set() method and an Integer object is expected in the get() method, then a run time exception will be thrown.

In class2, Generics is used and any non-primitive type can be used in the place of type T. Setting and getting different objects for type T will throw a compile time error.

5.1.3

```
public class Spacecraft<T> {

    private T t;
    public void set(T t) { this.t = t; }
    public T get() {return t;}
}
```

In the above code, Spacecraft class uses Generics and type variable T can be replaced by any non-primitive type like

a. Class or Interface
b. Array
c. Another type variable
d. All of the above

Ans: d

Answer Explanation:

Generic type invocation replaces T with some concrete value which can be a Class, Interface, Array or a different type variable.

Following line can be used to instantiate this class

Spacecraft<String> spacecraft = new Spacecraft<String>();

This is very similar to the ArrayList instantiation.

List<Integer> arrList = new ArrayList<Integer>();

The Collections classes use Generics heavily.

5.2 ANNOTATION

5.2.1

```
@SuppressWarnings("unchecked")
public someMethod() {
      ------
}
@Override
public someOtherMethod() {
      ------
}
```

Above are simple annotations that are commonly used. Annotations are used for

a. providing information for compiler
b. compile-time or deployment-time processing
c. run-time processing
d. all of the above

Ans: d

Answer Explanation:

Annotation is metadata that provides data about code. Annotations have no direct effect on the operation of the code they annotate.

Annotations can be used by compilers to suppress warnings and can be processed to generate code.

```
@Override
public someOtherMethod() {
      ------
}
```

The @ sign indicates to the compiler that this is an annotation. Name of the above annotation is Override. @Override annotation informs the compiler that this method is overriding the method in the super class.

5.2.2

Annotations can be applied to a

a. Class
b. Field
c. Method
d. All of the above

Ans: d

Answer Explanation:

Annotations can be applied to classes, fields, methods and other program elements.

5.3 ENUM TYPES

5.3.1

```
public class Direction {

    public static final int NORTH = 0;
    public static final int SOUTH = 1;
    public static final int EAST = 2;
    public static final int WEST = 3;

    public static void main(String [] args) {

        int curDir = Direction.NORTH;
    }
}
public class EnumDemo {

    public enum Direction {NORTH, SOUTH, EAST, WEST}

    public static void main(String [] args) {

        Direction curDir = Direction.NORTH;
    }
}
```

From the above sample code, which of the following statements on enum data type are true?

a. enums are easy to read and compiler can catch errors
b. enum variable can be set to one of the predefined constant value
c. enum constants are implicitly static and final
d. all of the above

Ans: d

Answer Explanation:

If a String or an integer value is used in place of enum type, it is usually difficult to read and is possible to have wrong assignments for the values that cannot be caught at compile time.

For the above example, the following two values are wrong and cannot be caught at compile time if the value was represented as an int or a String literal.

int curDir = 5;
String curDir = "NORTH EAST"

Using enum helps catch bugs at compile-time and reduces bugs in the code. Enum type can be used whenever a fixed set of constants need to be represented.

The enum declaration defines a class, and the class body can include methods and other fields. The constructor of an enum type must be declared private or package-private and enum class cannot be instantiated.

5.3.2

```
public class EnumDemo {

    public enum Season {

        SPRING("green", "cool"),
        SUMMER("brown", "hot"),
        FALL("yellow", "humid"),
        WINTER("white", "cold");

        private final String color;
        private final String temperature;

        Season(String color, String temperature) {

            this.color = color;
            this.temperature = temperature;
        }
        public String color() { return color;}

        public String temperature() { return temperature;}
    }
```

```
        public static void main(String [] args) {
            for (Season s : Season.values()) {
                System.out.println(s + " color is " + s.color() + " and
                temperature is " + s.temperature());
            }
        }
    }
```

Output:

SPRING color is green and temperature is cool
SUMMER color is brown and temperature is hot
FALL color is yellow and temperature is humid
WINTER color is white and temperature is cold

In the above code, enum constants are declared with values for the following parameters

a. color
b. temperature
c. all of the above
d. none of the above

Ans: c

Answer Explanation:

The enum type Season in the above example represents the four seasons. The enum constants are defined with the color and temperature parameters.

The enum Season declaration in the above example defines a class. The class body above, includes methods color() and temperature() along with the fields color and temperature.

The static values() method in the enhanced for loop returns the array of all the values of the enum in the order they are declared.

CORE JAVA ADVANCED

Collections

6.1 COLLECTION FRAMEWORK BASICS

6.1.1

Which of the following interfaces extend Collection interface?

a. List and Map
b. Set and Map
c. List, Set, and Map
d. List and Set

Ans: d

Answer Explanation:

List and Set interfaces extend Collection interface. Collection interface is the root interface for the entire Collection framework. All Collection classes implement Collection interface through one of the sub interfaces like List, Set or Queue. Map interface does not extend the Collection interface.

6.1.2

1. List is a ordered collection that allows duplicates while Set is a unordered collection without duplicates.
2. List does not maintain insertion order while Set maintains insertion order.
3. List maintains insertion order while Set does not maintains insertion order.
4. List allows positional access while Set does not.

Which of the above statements are correct regarding List and Set?

a. 1,3, and 4
b. 2 and 4
c. 1,2, and 3
d. 1,2,3, and 4

Ans: a

COLLECTION FRAMEWORK BASICS

Answer Explanation:

List is an ordered collection which means the elements in a list are stored in a specific order. In an ArrayList the order for the elements are maintained by the index position.

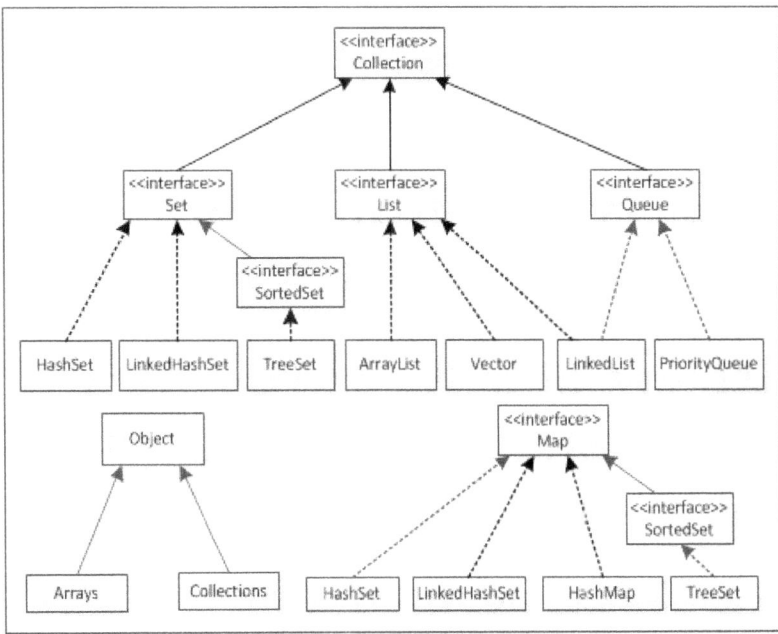

Set is an unordered collection and does not allow duplicates. All elements in a Set are unique. When add() method is used to insert a new element in the Set, equals() method is used to check if the element is already present. The element is added only if it is not already present in the Set.

6.1.3

Difference between Collection and Collections

a. Collection is an interface and Collections is a class with static utility methods.

b. Collections is an interface and Collection is a class with static utility methods.
c. Collection and Collections are both interfaces.
d. Collection and Collections are both classes with static utility methods.

Ans: a

Answer Explanation:

List, Set, and Queue are sub interfaces of Collection interface. Map interface does not extend the Collection interface.

Collection interface has methods such as size(), add(), remove(), iterator() which are implemented by the Collection classes. Collection classes implement Collection interface through one of the sub interfaces listed above.

Collections is a class with static utility methods that work with Collection objects. Examples of Collections utility functions are

Collections.synchronizedSet(Set s)
Collections.synchronizedMap(Map m)
Collections.synchronizedList(List l)

Collections.unmodifiableSet(Set s)
Collections.unmodifiableMap(Map m)
Collections.unmodifiableList(List l)

Collections.min(Collection c)
Collections.max(Collection c)
Collections.copy(List to, List from)

Collections.reverse(List l)
Collections.sort(List l)
Collections.shuffle(List l)

6.2 ARRAYS, ARRAYLIST AND LINKEDLIST

6.2.1

ArrayList and Vector

a. All methods of Vector are synchronized while ArrayList methods are not synchronized.
b. ArrayList is faster than Vector since Vector is synchronized.
c. Vector is a legacy class that is obsolete.
d. All of the above

Ans: d

Answer Explanation:

Vector is a legacy class and may not be supported in future JDK versions, so it's better to use ArrayList. If synchronization is needed, the ArrayList can be wrapped using Collections.synchronizedList().

6.2.2

public static final List myList;

In the above declaration, myList is declared final, which means it cannot be altered, but this is a mutable object that can be changed using mutator methods like add(), remove() etc. How can myList be made final in the real sense?

a. Make this variable private and assign Collections.unmodifiableList(list) for this variable.
b. Make this variable private and wrap the accessor methods to return Collections.unmodifiableList(myList)
c. All of the above
d. None of the above

Ans: c

Answer Explanation:

If a mutable object is declared final, it's still not final as the mutator method can be used to change the state of the object. To make any of the Collection to be final, the following methods of the Collections class can be used.

Collections.unmodifiableCollection(Collection c)
Collections.unmodifiableList(List l)
Collections.unmodifiableSet(Set s)
Collections.unmodifiableMap(Map m)

The above methods return unmodifiable view of the Collection, List, Set or Map that is passed as a parameter. These views that are returned are also called wrappers because they wrap the original Collection.

These wrappers add runtime checks to the original Collection and throw a UnsupportedOperationException if any of the mutator methods are accessed.

6.2.3

Difference between Array and ArrayList

1. Arrays have fixed size while ArrayList have dynamic size, keeps growing if needed.
2. Array can contain Objects and primitive types while ArrayList can have only Objects as elements.
3. While creating an instance of ArrayList, it's not necessary to specify the size but for Array, the size needs to be specified.
4. For adding or getting elements, ArrayList is slightly faster than Arrays.
5. ArrayList resize operation may slow down performance.

a. All of the above statements are true
b. All except 4 are true
c. All except 5 are true
d. All except 4 and 5 are true

Ans: b

Answer Explanation:

ARRAYS, ARRAYLIST AND LINKEDLIST

Following is an array declaration:

int [] array = new int[10];
array[10] = 2;

While declaring an array, the size of the array should be specified. Array has fixed length, once the size is specified, it cannot be changed. If the array index accessed exceeds the capacity as shown above, ArrayIndexOutOfBoundsException is thrown. Since the size of the array is 10, the indexes from 0 to 9 are valid and 10 is not a valid index.

List<Integer> arrayList2 = new ArrayList<Integer>(1);
arrayList2.add(10);
arrayList2.add(20);
arrayList2.add(30);
System.*out*.println("arrayList2: " + arrayList2);

Output:

arrayList2: [10, 20, 30]

Size of the ArrayList is optional and need not be specified. When the size is specified as 1 and is exceeded as shown above, the size of the ArrayList is increased internally. ArrayList has dynamic allocation of more memory when more elements are being added and the size of the existing allocated memory is not enough.

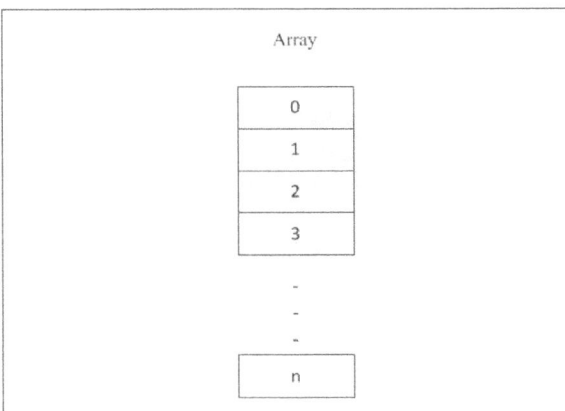

Array resize operation may slow down performance as a new ArrayList with a larger capacity is created and all the elements from the existing ArrayList is copied to the new one.

Array can take primitive types like int or objects, while ArrayList takes only objects like String, Integer etc. For adding and getting elements, Arrays are faster than ArrayList.

6.2.4

Difference between ArrayList and LinkedList

1. If an element is removed or added in an ArrayList, all elements after this element should be moved up or down.
2. ArrayList and Array store objects in consecutive memory locations while LinkedList stores objects in seperate links with one object having a reference to the next link.
3. LinkedList is faster in add and remove but slower in get, compared to ArrayList.
4. LinkedList has more memory overhead than ArrayList as LinkedList stores both the data and address of next and previous nodes.

a. All of the above statements are true.
b. All except 3 are true
c. All except 4 are true
d. All except 3 and 4 are true

Ans: a

Answer Explanation:

```
List<String> arrayList = new ArrayList<String>();
arrayList.add("a");
arrayList.add("b");
arrayList.add("c");

LinkedList linkedList = new LinkedList();
linkedList.add("a");
linkedList.add("b");
linkedList.add("c");
```

linkedList.remove("a");
System.*out*.println("arrayList: " + arrayList);
System.*out*.println("arrayList.get(0): " + arrayList.get(0));
System.*out*.println("linkedList: " + linkedList);

Output:

arrayList: [a, b, c]
arrayList.get(0): a
linkedList: bc

ArrayList and LinkedList implement the List interface in which elements are ordered.

ArrayList stores memory in contiguous memory location. If an element is removed from the middle of the ArrayList, all the other elements have to be moved up. Same issue is with inserting an element. This makes adding and removing elements in the middle of an ArrayList expensive.

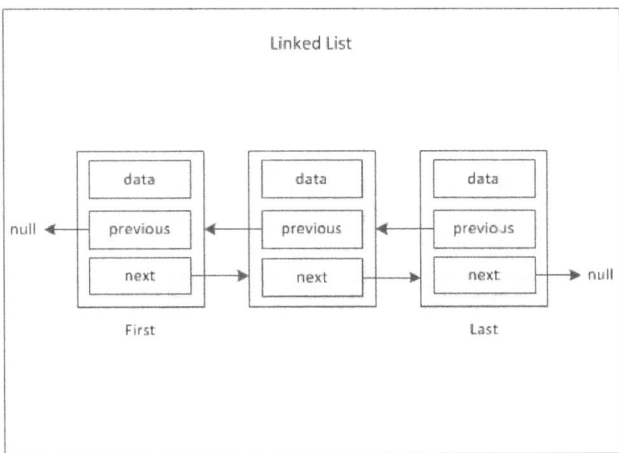

LinkedList stores the elements in a separate link and each link also has a reference to the next link. Insertion and deletion in the middle of the link is not expensive. When an element is removed, simply the reference of the previous link is changed.

In Java, LinkedList is a doubly linked list, each link has a reference to the next and previous link.

If the application requires adding all the elements once and then a lot of random access based on index and doesn't have frequent inserts or deletes, ArrayList can be used. If there are more inserts and deletes than access to elements, LinkedList can be used.

6.2.5

If you need to access random elements using indexes, which of the following will you use?

a. ArrayList
b. LinkedList
c. HashSet
d. HashMap

Ans: a

Answer Explanation:

ArrayList maintains the order for the elements by index position.

Since ArrayList saves the elements in contiguous memory, every time an element is added or removed from the middle of the list, all the other elements have to be moved down or up. This makes add and delete operation in ArrayList expensive.

If there is not much of add and delete operations, but more of access operations using the index position, then ArrayList can be used.

```
List<String> arrayList = new ArrayList<String>();
arrayList.add("a");
arrayList.add("b");
arrayList.add("c");

System.out.println("arrayList: " + arrayList);
System.out.println("arrayList.get(0): " + arrayList.get(0));
System.out.println("arrayList.get(1): " + arrayList.get(1));
```

Output:

arrayList: [a, b, c]
arrayList.get(0): a
arrayList.get(1): b

6.2.6

1. Before Java 5

List<Integer> seatList = new ArrayList<Integer> ();

seatList.add(0, new Integer(27));
int seatNumber = seatList.get(0).intValue();

2. Java 5 and later

List<Integer> seatList = new ArrayList<Integer> ();

seatList.add(0,27);
int seatNumber = seatList.get(0);

In the code snippet 2, for add operations of seatList, the primitive int is automatically converted into object Integer. In the get operation, Integer is automatically converted into int. This is possible because of

a. Typecasting
b. Autoboxing
c. Reflection
d. Generics

Ans: b

Answer Explanation:

Collections can hold objects and not primitives. So prior to Java 5, primitives had to be wrapped using wrapper class to create a corresponding object before passing to Collection classes. Now, autoboxing handles this converting from primitive to object and object to primitive. Example of some of the wrapper classes are Integer, Double, Float, Long, Short, and Boolean.

6.3 HASHSET, HASHMAP AND CONCURRENT HASHMAP

6.3.1

HashTable is a

a. Array
b. LinkedList
c. Array of LinkedList
d. ArrayList

Ans: c

Answer Explanation:

The hash table is an array of linked lists. Each list is called a bucket.

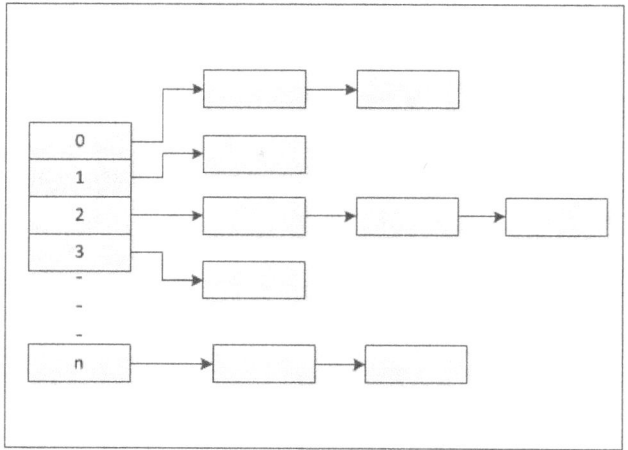

Hash table is a data structure for finding objects quickly. The hash table computes an integer called hashcode for each object using the hashCode() function provided by either the object (eg: String object) or its base class, Object.

Once hash code is computed, hash code modulo the total number of buckets gives the index of the bucket where the element should be stored.

If the hash code of the object is 449 and the total number of buckets is 121, the reminder of 449 divided by 121 gives 71. So the object is placed in bucket 71.

If there is no other element in this bucket, then the object is inserted. If there are elements already in this bucket, it's called hash collision. The new object has to be compared with all the objects in the bucket to check if there is a match to avoid duplicate key entries.

If the hash codes are randomly distributed and if the number of buckets are large enough, then few hash comparisons will be needed.

6.3.2

For a hash table, the 'initial capacity' is the initial number of buckets, 'load factor' is the measure of how full the hash table is allowed to get. The default load factor value is .75

If the number of elements for a HashTable is 100, how much should be the initial capacity for the HashTable.

a. 100
b. 50
c. 140
d. 200

Ans: c

Answer Explanation:

$100/140 = .71$ which is close to the default recommended load factor value of .75

6.3.3

Difference between HashMap and HashSet

1. HashMap stores key/value pair while HashSet stores only the value.
2. Duplicate values are allowed for HashMap but not for HashSet.
3. For HashMap, hash code value is calculated using key object, while for HashSet, hashcode value is calculated using value object.
4. Both allow null values and are not synchronized.

Which of the above statements are true?

a. All except 3
b. All except 4
c. All except 3 and 4
d. All of the above

Ans: d

Answer Explanation:

```
Set<String> hSet = new HashSet<String>();
hSet.add("a");
hSet.add("b");
hSet.add("c");
hSet.add("a");
hSet.add(null);
System.out.println("hSet: " + hSet);

Map<Integer, String> hMap = new HashMap<Integer, String>();
hMap.put(1, "a");
hMap.put(2, "b");
hMap.put(3, "c");
hMap.put(4, "a");
hMap.put(null, null);
System.out.println("hMap: " + hMap);
```

Output:

hSet: [null, b, c, a]
hMap: {null=null, 1=a, 2=b, 3=c, 4=a}

HASHSET, HASHMAP AND CONCURRENT HASHMAP

In the above sample, HashSet takes only values and HashMap takes key/value pairs. Both HashSet and HashMap take null values.

When duplicate value a is added to hSet, it is not stored. When duplicate value a is put in hMap with key 4, it is stored with that key as shown in the output.

HashSet implements the Set interface and HashMap the Map interface. Both Set and Map are unordered collections.

Set stores only values while Map stores key/value pairs. Set does not allow duplicate values while Map allows duplicate values.

When add() method is used to insert a new element, equals() method is used to check if the element is already present in the Set. If the element is already present, it's not added.

For HashSet, hashcode is computed using the value object and for HashMap using key object.

6.3.4

Difference between HashMap and Hashtable

a. HashMap is faster than Hashtable, as Hashtable is synchronized and HashMap is not
b. HashMap allows null values while Hashtable does not
c. Hashtable class is obsolete and ConcurrentHashMap should be used in its place
d. All of the above

Ans: d

Answer Explanation:

Hashtable is synchronized, as a result thread-safe and HashMap is not.

Since Hashtable is obsolete, if HashMap needs to be used in a multi-threaded environment its accessor methods can be synchronized using the static method synchronizedMap() in the Collections class.

Map m = Collections.*synchronizedMap*(hashMap);

Also ConcurretHashMap can be used as it is synchronized and is faster than Hashtable and synchronizedMap. ConcurretHashMap locks only portion of the Map instead of the whole Map like Hashtable or synchronizedMap.

ConcurrentHashMap has memory and processor overhead and should be used only in highly concurrent applications. For others, synchronized HashMap is a better choice.

6.3.5

Difference between ConcurrentHashMap, Hashtable, and synchronizedMap

1. ConcurrentHashMap is faster than Hashtable or synchronizedMap.
2. ConcurrentHashMap locks only portion of the Map instead of the whole Map like Hashtable or synchronizedMap
3. ConcurrentHashMap is best suited for a multi-threaded environment with multiple readers and few writers.
4. ConcurrentHashMap allows null as key or value.

Which of the above statements are true?

a. All except 3
b. All except 4
c. All except 3 and 4
d. All of the above

Ans: b

Answer Explanation:

Hashtable is a synchronized collection class and is obsolete.

Collections.synchronizedMap() returns an instance of a synchronized wrapper class.

Map synchMap = Collections.*synchronizedMap*(hashMap);

The static synchronizedMap() method of the Collections class turns hashMap into a synchronized Map, synchMap with all the accessor methods synchronized. The synchronized get() and put() methods acquire a lock on synchMap.

synchMap is an object of a class that implements the Map interface and whose methods manipulate the methods of the original Map. This is called a view or a wrapper.

While iterating through synchMap, it needs to be synchronized, this is because only the accessor methods of the Map interface are synchronized but the original Collection object is not.

Also in a multi threaded environment, while iterating through any map, an object level lock should be acquired, otherwise if any other thread tries to modify the map at the same time, ConcurrentModification Exception is thrown.

```
synchronized(synchMap) {

    Iterator iter = synchMap.iterator();
    while(iter.hasNext()) {
    ...
    }
}
```

Locking this entire collection is a performance overhead, when one method acquires a lock on synchMap, other methods cannot access it. ConcurrentHashMap solves this problem by providing fine grain locking and not holding a lock on the entire Map, so concurrent reads and writes are possible.

ConcurrentHashMap does not throw a ConcurrentModification Exception when a thread is iterating over it and another thread modifies the hashMap at the same time. This is because the iterator returned by ConcurrentHashMap is a snapshot of the data.
ConcurrentHashMap is designed for highly concurrent applications.

ConcurrentHashMap allows different threads to access different parts of the Map simultaneously. The Map is split internally into multiple parts depending on the concurrency level specified in the constructor. The default value of 16 for concurrency level will allow 16 concurrent updates on the hashMap.

As indicated above, ConcurrentHashMap has a lot of overhead in terms of memory and processor and should be used only in highly concurrent applications. For others, synchronized HashMap is a better choice.

6.3.6

To preserve the order of the elements in the sequence they are inserted, the following Collection can be used:

a. Set
b. SortedSet
c. LinkedHashSet
d. TreeSet

Ans: c

Answer Explanation:

LinkedHashSet maintains the insertion order.

```
Set<String> hSet = new HashSet<String>();
hSet.add("a");
hSet.add("b");
hSet.add("c");
hSet.add("d");
hSet.add(null);
System.out.println("hSet: " + hSet);

Set<String> lhSet = new LinkedHashSet<String>();
lhSet.add("a");
lhSet.add("b");
lhSet.add("c");
lhSet.add("d");
lhSet.add(null);
System.out.println("lhSet: " + lhSet);
```

Output:
hSet: [null, d, b, c, a]
lhSet: [a, b, c, d, null]

Both HashSet and LinkedHashSet implement the Set interface and don't allow duplicates. They allow null values as shown above and both use equals() method for comparison. HashSet internally uses HashMap and LinkedHashSet internally uses LinkedHashMap.

HashSet is faster than LinkedHashSet as LinkedHashSet has to maintain a doubly linked list for insert and delete.

6.4 HASHCODE AND EQUALS

6.4.1

hashCode() and equals() methods are defined in the following class

a. Object
b. Class
c. Thread
d. Iterator

Ans: a

Answer Explanation:

hashCode() and equals() methods are defined in the Object class.
Object is the super class for all objects on java. All objects are direct or indirect descendents of the Object class and as a result, all objects inherit the methods of the Object class.

6.4.2

hashCode() method of the Object class derives the hash code from the object's

a. Memory address
b. Content
c. Reference
d. Value

Ans: a

Answer Explanation:

Object.hashCode() usually returns the memory address of the object.

From Java API documentation for java.lang.Object

"As much as is reasonably practical, the hashCode method defined by class Object does return distinct integers for distinct objects. (This is

typically implemented by converting the internal address of the object into an integer, but this implementation technique is not required by the JavaTM programming language.)"

The general contract for hashCode is

1. If invoked on the same object, more than once, the hashCode method should consistently return the same integer.

2. If two objects are equal according to equals(Object) method, then hashCode methods on each of these two objects should produce the same integer result.

3. If two objects are unequal according to equals(Object) method, then different integer results need not be produced by hashCode methods.

6.4.3

```
String str1 = "Hello";
StringBuffer strBuff1 = new StringBuffer(str1);

System.out.println("str1 hashCode: " + str1.hashCode());
System.out.println("strBuff1 hashCode: " + strBuff1.hashCode());

String str2 = "Hello";
StringBuffer strBuff2 = new StringBuffer(str2);

System.out.println("str2 hashCode: " + str2.hashCode());
System.out.println("strBuff2 hashCode: " + strBuff2.hashCode());
```

Running the above code snippet prints the following result:

str1 hashCode: 69609650
strBuff1 hashCode: 2017815052

str2 hashCode: 69609650
strBuff2 hashCode: 355825540

The hashCode value for different instances of String "Hello" is always the same while the hashCode value for different instances of StringBuffer "Hello" are different, because

a. hashCode is computed in the String class using the content, while StringBuffer uses hashCode method from Object class that is computed from the memory location.
b. Different instances of String value of "Hello" represent the same content while StringBuffer represents different contents.
c. Both String and StringBuffer use hashCode computed in the Object method, but since String value is represented by the same memory location, they are the same.
d. None of the above

Ans: a

Answer Explanation:

Object is the super class for all objects in java. All objects are direct or indirect descendents of the Object class and as a result, all objects inherit the method hashCode() of the Object class.

hashCode() method of Object class returns the memory address of the object.

StringBuffer class doesn't have its own implementation of the hashCode() method, so the hashCode() method of the Object class is used. For same value "Hello", two StringBuffer instances return two different hashCodes as the memory addresses are different.

String class overrides the hashCode() method of the Object class with its own implementation to return a hash code value depending on the string value. As a result, two String objects with the same content return the same hash code value.

Generating hashcode using a function or an algorithm to map an object data to an integer value is called hashing.

6.4.4

If hashCode() method is not defined for a class, then two objects of this class with same content added to a HashSet will have

a. same hash code

b. different hash codes
c. random hash codes
d. correct hash code

Ans: b

Answer Explanation:

If hashCode() method is not defined for a class, the hashCode() method of the Object class will be used. The default implementation of hashCode() method by Object class, is derived by mapping the object's memory address to an integer value.

The two objects having the same content will have different hash codes as the memory address of them are different.

6.4.5

equals() method of the Object class checks equality of two objects by comparing the

a. identity
b. content
c. reference
d. memory address

Ans: d

Answer Explanation:

equals() method in Object class returns true if two non null objects refer to the same object. In the Object class, implementation of equals class looks like this:

public boolean equals(Object obj) {

    if(obj == null) {
        return false;
    }
    return (this == obj);
}

When the equals() method is overridden, the general contract should be followed. Following is the contract from the Java API documentation for java.lang.Object

"The equals method implements an equivalence relation on non-null object references:

It is reflexive: for any non-null reference value x, x.equals(x) should return true.

It is symmetric: for any non-null reference values x and y, x.equals(y) should return true if and only if y.equals(x) returns true.

It is transitive: for any non-null reference values x, y, and z, if x.equals(y) returns true and y.equals(z) returns true, then x.equals(z) should return true.

It is consistent: for any non-null reference values x and y, multiple invocations of x.equals(y) consistently return true or consistently return false, provided no information used in equals comparisons on the objects is modified.

For any non-null reference value x, x.equals(null) should return false. "

Whenever the equals() method is overridden, it's necessary to override the hashCode() method also to maintain the general contract of hashCode which states that equal objects should have equal hash codes.

6.4.6

Which of the following should implement equals() and hashCode() methods?

a. An Object that is used as a key or value in a Map or Set.
b. An Object that is used in any Collection.
c. An Object that is used as a key in a Map and value in a Set.
d. An Object used as a value in any Collection.

Ans: c

Answer Explanation:

HASHCODE AND EQUALS

The Object that is used for hashing in the Map or Set should implement equals() and hashCode() methods. Key is hashed in the Map and value is hashed in the Set. So the objects that are used as key in Map and value in Set should define the equals() and hashCode() methods.

6.4.7

```java
public class Aircraft {

    String name;
    Date startTime;

    public Aircraft(String n , Date d) {
        name = n;
        startTime = d;
    }
    public int hashCode() {

        int result = 15;
        result = 37 * result + name.hashCode();
        result = 37 * result + startTime.hashCode();
        return result;
    }
    public boolean equals(Object other) {

        if ((other != null) && (getClass() == other.getClass())) {

            Aircraft otherCraft = (Aircraft) other;

            return (name.equals(otherCraft.name) &&
                    (startTime.equals(otherCraft.startTime)));
        }
        return false;
    }

    public static void main(String [] args) {

        Date d = new Date();

        Map<Aircraft, String> hMap =
            new HashMap<Aircraft, String>();
```

```
        hMap.put(new Aircraft("Boeing 727", d), "passenger craft");

        String acStr=
            (String) hMap.get(new Aircraft("Boeing 727", d));

        System.out.println("acStr: " + acStr);
    }
}
```

For the above code snippet hashCode() and equals() are defined, hMap.get() will return the following

a. null
b. passenger craft
c. empty string
d. Boeing 727

Ans: b

Answer Explanation:

Since both hashCode() and equals() method for the Aircraft class have been defined correctly, the put() and get() methods of hMap use these functions to save and retrieve equal instances of Aircraft class.

hashCode() method is used during put to compute the hash code value and save the object in the correct hash bucket. When hMap.get() is called, hashCode() method is used to compute the hash code value for an equal instance of Aircraft which will result in an equal hash code value.

During hMap.get(), for the hash bucket, when equals() method is invoked on these two equal Aircraft objects with equal hash code values, it returns true and the correct value is retrieved. For computing the hash code shown above, 15 is an arbitrary number and 37 is an odd prime.

In the above sample code, name and startTime are not made private for simplicity. When access modifier is not specified, default is protected access for the class and sub-classes.

6.4.8

```java
public class Aircraft {
    String name;
    Date startTime;

    public Aircraft(String n , Date d) {
        name = n;
        startTime = d;
    }

    public boolean equals(Object other) {

        if ((other != null) && (getClass() == other.getClass())) {

            Aircraft otherCraft = (Aircraft) other;

            return (name.equals(otherCraft.name) &&
                        (startTime.equals(otherCraft.startTime)));
        }
        return false;
    }

    public static void main(String [] args) {

        Date d = new Date();

        Map<Aircraft, String> hMap =
            new HashMap<Aircraft, String>();

        hMap.put(new Aircraft("Boeing 727", d), "passenger craft");

        String acStr=
            (String) hMap.get(new Aircraft("Boeing 727", d));

        System.out.println("acStr: " + acStr);
    }
}
```

For the above code snippet only equals() method is defined and not hashCode() method, hMap.get() will return the following

a. null
b. passenger craft
c. empty string
d. Boeing 727

Ans: a

Answer Explanation:

Since hashCode() method is not implemented for the Aircraft class, the hashCode() method from Object class will be used. The hashCode() method of the Object class returns the memory address of the object.

This will return different values for hash code values for equal instances in put() and get() methods, as a result of which the value saved is not found by the get() method and a null value is returned.

Whenever equals() is implemented, hashCode() should be implemented to maintain the general contract of hashCode which states that equal objects should have equals hashCodes.

6.4.9

```
public class Aircraft {

    String name;
    Date startTime;

    public Aircraft(String n , Date d) {
        name = n;
        startTime = d;
    }

    public int hashCode() {

        int result = 17;
        result = 37 * result + name.hashCode();
        result = 37 * result + startTime.hashCode();
        return result;
    }
```

HASHCODE AND EQUALS

```
public static void main(String [] args) {

    Date d = new Date();

    Map<Aircraft, String> hMap =
        new HashMap<Aircraft, String>();
    hMap.put(new Aircraft("Boeing 727", d), "passenger craft");

    String acStr=
        (String) hMap.get(new Aircraft("Boeing 727", d));

    System.out.println("acStr: " + acStr);
    }
}
```

For the above code snippet, only hashCode() method is defined and not equals(), hMap.get() will return the following

a. null
b. passenger craft
c. empty string
d. Boeing 727

Ans: a

Answer Explanation:

When get() and put() methods of hMap call hashCode() method on equal instances of Aircraft, it returns the same hash code value for both. Since both hash code values are same, the equals() method is called within the same hash bucket to check for equality of the objects.

Since equals() method is not implemented for the Aircraft class, the equals() method from Object class will be used.

The equals() method of the Object class will return false when two equal instances of Aircraft are compared. This is because the equals() method of Object class compares if the two objects have the same memory address. As a result, the value saved is not retrieved by get() and returns a null value.

The equals() method should be overridden with the correct implementation, for proper functioning of HashMap and HashSet with the object.

6.5 TREESET AND TREEMAP

6.5.1

Difference between HashMap and TreeMap

1. HashMap elements are stored in a hash table while TreeMap elements are stored in a tree.
2. HashMap is unsorted, there is no ordering of key or values, while TreeMap is sorted and the elements are ordered by keys.
3. Adding an element to HashMap is faster than adding to TreeMap.
4. Keys added to HashMap should have hashCode() implementation while the keys added to TreeMap should be sortable, which can be specified in a comparator interface

Which of the above statements are true?

a. All except 3
b. All except 4
c. All of the above
d. None of the above

Ans: c

Answer Explanation:

Map<String, String> hMap = new HashMap<String, String>();
hMap.put("a", "a");
hMap.put("b", "b");
hMap.put("c", "c");
hMap.put("d", "d");

for(String value : hMap.values()) {
    System.*out*.println("HasMap value: " + value);
}

Map<String, String> tMap = new TreeMap<String, String>();
tMap.put("c", "c");
tMap.put("b", "b");
tMap.put("d", "d");
tMap.put("a", "a");

```
for(String value : tMap.values()) {
    System.out.println("TreeMap value: " + value);
}
```

Output:

HasMap value: d
HasMap value: b
HasMap value: c
HasMap value: a

TreeMap value: a
TreeMap value: b
TreeMap value: c
TreeMap value: d

Both HashMap and TreeMap implement the Map interface and are not synchronized. Both don't allow duplicate keys. HashMap allows null values for key and value while TreeMap allows null for value only.

HashMap is implemented as a hash table. HashMap is an unordered collection used when ordering of the elements doesn't matter and provides fast lookup.

The elements in a TreeMap are stored in a tree and the elements can be retrieved in a sorted order as specified using the Comparable or Comparator interface. TreeMap is slower than HashMap.

6.5.2

```
public class Aircraft implements Comparable {

    String name;
    Date startTime;

    public Aircraft(String n) {
        this(n, new Date());
    }

    public Aircraft(String n , Date d) {
        name = n;
```

```
            startTime = d;
        }

        public int compareTo(Object other) {

            Aircraft otherCraft = (Aircraft) other;

            return name.compareTo(otherCraft.name);
        }
}
```

Since the Aircraft class implements Comparable interface and has compareTo() method implemented, instance of Aircraft can be saved in sorted order in a

a. Array
b. ArrayList
c. HashMap
d. TreeSet

Ans: d

Answer Explanation:

```
public static void main(String [] args) {

    TreeSet<Aircraft> tSet = new TreeSet<Aircraft> ();

    tSet.add(new Aircraft("Whirlwind"));
    tSet.add(new Aircraft("Aurora"));
    tSet.add(new Aircraft("Thunderjet"));

    for(Aircraft craft : tSet) {
        System.out.println(craft.getName());
    }
}
```

Output:

Aurora
Thunderjet
Whirlwind

In the above sample, the compareTo() method implements the ordering of Aircraft objects according to the name. Inside main, when the Aircraft objects are added to the TreeSet, they are stored in the sorted order as shown in the output.

Comparable interface is used to implement natural ordering of objects, it has one method

public int compareTo(Object other)

a.compareTo(b) returns zero if a and b are equal, 1 if a is greater than b, -1 if a is lesser than b in the sort order. In the above sample, compareTo method of String class is used.

Objects that implement Comparable interface can be used as keys in TreeMap or TreeSet. Also, list or array of these objects can be used in Collections.sort and Arrays.sort for sorting.

6.5.3

```
public static void main(String [] args) {

    TreeSet<Aircraft> tSet =
    new TreeSet<Aircraft>(new Comparator<Aircraft>() {

        @Override
        public int compare(Aircraft a, Aircraft b){

            return a.getName().compareTo(b.getName());
        }
    });

    tSet.add(new Aircraft("Whirlwind"));
    tSet.add(new Aircraft("Aurora"));
    tSet.add(new Aircraft("Thunderjet"));
    tSet.add(new Aircraft("Starlifter"));

    for(Aircraft craft : tSet) {

        System.out.println(craft.getName());
    }
```

}
The above code when run, prints the Aircraft objects sorted by

a. Date
b. Time
c. Name
d. None of the above

Ans: c

Output:

Aurora
Starlifter
Thunderjet
Whirlwind

Answer Explanation:

Comparator interface can be used to define the sort order on the fly, when the object added to TreeSet does not implement the Comparable interface. Also, if the Aircraft object needs to be sorted by name sometimes and Date sometimes, then Comparator interface can be used. The Comparator interface has one method

public int compare(Aircraft a, Aircraft b)

Similar to compareTo() method, compare() method returns zero if a and b are equal, 1 if a is greater than b, -1 if a is lesser than b in the sort order.

The Comparator object is usually defined on the fly as an anonymous inner class for convenience, since it's used only for defining the compare method. The Comparator object is passed to the TreeSet constructor and is used for determining the sort order as shown in the sample above. Below is a sample for using comparator with Collections.sort().

public static void sortAircraftAnonymous(List<Aircraft> aircraft) {

    Collections.*sort*(aircraft, new Comparator<Aircraft>() {

        @Override

```
            public int compare(Aircraft x, Aircraft y) {
                int difference =
                        x.getModelNumber() - y.getModelNumber();

                if (difference < 0) return -1;
                if (difference > 0) return 1;

                return 0;
            }
        });
}
```

6.5.4

If the key value specified in get() method is not found in a HashMap the following value is returned

a. null
b. empty string
c. random value
d. none of the above

Ans: a

Answer Explanation:

If the key passed to the get() method of HashMap is not found, then null is returned.

Map<Integer, String> hMap = new HashMap<Integer, String>();

hMap.put(1, "a");
hMap.put(2, "b");
hMap.put(3, "c");
hMap.put(4, "d");

System.*out*.println("hMap.get(5): " + hMap.get(5));

Output:

hMap.get(5): null

6.5.5

Map<String, Aircraft> hMap = new HashMap<String, Aircraft>();

hMap.put("34892", new Aircraft("Boeing 727"));

If the key value 34892 is already present in hMap with an existing value:

a. the existing value remains unchanged.
b. new value in the put method replaces the existing value.
c. put method is not executed.
d. none of the above.

Ans: b

Answer Explanation:

Map<Integer, String> hMap = new HashMap<Integer, String>();

hMap.put(1, "a");
hMap.put(2, "b");
hMap.put(3, "c");
hMap.put(4, "d");
System.*out*.println("hMap: " + hMap);

hMap.put(1, "z");
System.*out*.println("hMap: " + hMap);

Output:

hMap: {1=a, 2=b, 3=c, 4=d}
hMap: {1=z, 2=b, 3=c, 4=d}

In the above sample, when key value pair of 1 and z are added to hMap using put() method, z replaces the existing value a.

6.6 VIEWS AND WRAPPERS

6.6.1

Map hMap = new HashMap();

Map synchMap = Collections.synchronizedMap(hMap);

In the above code snippet, synchMap

a. Is an object of a class that implements Map interface with methods that wrap and manipulate the accessor methods of the original map.
b. has synchronized accessor methods like get() and put() that can be accessed from multiple threads.
c. all of the above
d. none of the above

Ans: c

Answer Explanation:

Collections.synchronizedMap() method returns an instance of a synchronized wrapper class.

Map synchMap = Collections.synchronizedMap(hMap);

synchMap is an object of a class that implements the Map interface and whose methods manipulate the methods of the original hMap. This is called a view or a wrapper.

The static synchronizedMap() method of the Collections class turns the hashMap into a synchronized map with all the accessor methods synchronized.

6.6.2

Map hMap = new HashMap();

Map sMap = Collections.synchronizedMap(hMap);

In the above code, sMap is thread safe. To make sure that no thread accesses the data structure through original unsynchronized access methods of hMap, following code snippet can be used:

a. Map sMap = Collections.synchronizedMap(new HashMap());
b. synchronized(hMap){...} ;
c. synchronized(sMap){...} ;
d. none of the above

Ans: a

Answer Explanation:

In the above code, sMap has all the accessor methods synchronized and is a wrapper for the original hMap. But the unsynchronized accessor methods are still accessible through hMap. The following initiation can be used to avoid this.

Map sMap = Collections.synchronizedMap(new HashMap());

In the above initiation, the original HashMap and its unsynchronized accessor methods will not be available.

6.6.3

Set sSet = Collections.synchronizedSet(new HashSet());

```
synchronized(sSet) {

        Iterator iter = sSet.iterator();

        while(iter.hasNext()) {
            ...
        }
}
```

In the above code snippet, does sSet need to be synchronized during iteration?

a. Yes, since sSet is not synchronized.
b. No, since sSet is already synchronized.

c. Yes, even though sSet is already synchronized.
d. None of the above.

Ans: a

Answer Explanation:

synchronizedSet() method returns an object that implements the Set interface and wraps the accessor methods of the original collection to make them synchronized. The original collection is not synchronized. So when the original collection is accessed using an iterator, the collection should be synchronized.

In a multi threaded environment, while iterating through a map, an object level lock should be acquired, otherwise if any other thread tries to modify the map at the same time, ConcurrentModificationException is thrown.

synchronized(synchMap) {

    Iterator iter = synchMap.iterator();

    while(iter.hasNext()) {

        ...
    }
}

6.6.4

List<Aircraft> acList = new ArrayList<Aircraft>();

List<Aircraft> uList = Collections.unmodifiableList(acList);

In the above code snippet, for uList

a. accessor methods are not supported
b. mutator methods are not supported
c. both accessor and mutator methods are not supported
d. all methods are supported

Ans: b

Answer Explanation:

Collections.unmodifiableList() method returns a wrapper to provide unmodifiable view of the collection.

Collections.unmodifiableList() method returns an object of a class that implements the List interface. All mutator methods for uList like add(), remove(), set() etc. throws UnsupportedOperationException.

This view can be used whenever the Collection needs to be accessed, but cannot be modified by another part of the code.

6.6.5

*Aircraft [] aircrafts = **new** Aircraft[20];*

List<Aircraft> aircraftList = Arrays.*asList*(aircrafts);

In the above code snippet,

1. aircraftList is not an ArrayList.
2. aircraftList is a view object with accessor methods accessing the underlying array.
3. Any aircraftList method that changes the size of the array like add and remove throws UnsupportedOperationException

Which of the above statements are true?

a. 2 and 3
b. 1 and 3
c. 1 and 2
d. 1, 2, and 3

Ans: d

Answer Explanation:

aircraftList object returned is not an instance of java.util.ArrayList but is an instance of java.util.Arrays$ArrayList class. This is ArrayList class which is a private static inner class of Arrays class.

aircraftList is a wrapper which wraps the get() and set() methods of the original Array. When add() and remove() methods are called, UnsupportedOperationException is thrown.

6.6.6

List dList = aList.subList(5, 10);
dList.clear();

In the above code snippet, dList.clear()

a. clears all elements of dList but doesn't affect aList
b. clears all elements of dList and clears the subList specified for aList
c. Does not clear dList or subList of aList
d. None of the above

Ans: b

Answer Explanation:

List<String> aList = new ArrayList<String>();
aList.add("a");
aList.add("b");
aList.add("c");
aList.add("d");

List dList = aList.subList(1, 3);

System.*out*.println("aList: " + aList + " dList: " + dList);

dList.clear();
System.*out*.println("After clearing, aList: " + aList + " dList: " + dList);

Output:

aList: [a, b, c, d] dList: [b, c]
After clearing, aList: [a, d] dList: []

In the above sample,

subList(int fromIndex, int toIndex)

is the signature of the subList() method that returns a sub list of the original list with fromIndex inclusive and toIndex exclusive.

From the original list aList, a subList dList is created with index 1 and 2 with values b and c. Then a call to dList.clear() clears the subList in both the dList and the original List aList.

dList is a view of the original List aList and hence the clear operation happens on both the lists. To clear sublist of the original list directly, the following statement can be used.

aList.subList(1, 3).clear();

6.6.7

Map<String, Aircraft> aircraftMap =
    new HashMap<String, Aircraft>();

Set<String> aircraftIdSet = new HashSet<String>();
....
....
aircraftMap.keySet().removeAll(aircraftIdSet);

The above snippet removes the aircraftIdSet elements from

a. aircraftMap
b. keyset
c. both
d. none of the above

Ans: a

Answer Explanation:

Since the keySet is a view to the map, the keys (aircraftId) and associated aircraft objects are removed from the map.

Map<Integer, String> hMap = new HashMap<Integer, String>();
hMap.put(1, "a");
hMap.put(2, "b");
hMap.put(3, "c");

```java
hMap.put(4, "d");
System.out.println("hMap: " + hMap);

Set<Integer> hSet = new HashSet<Integer>();
hSet.add(2);
hSet.add(3);
System.out.println("hSet: " + hSet);

hMap.keySet().removeAll(hSet);
System.out.println("After remove....");
System.out.println("hMap: " + hMap);
```

Output:

hMap: {1=a, 2=b, 3=c, 4=d}
hSet: [2, 3]
After remove....
hMap: {1=a, 4=d}

6.6.8

```java
Set xSet = ...;
Set ySet = ...;

Set zSet = new HashSet(xSet);
zSet.retainAll(ySet);
```

After executing the above code, zSet will have

a. Contents of xSet
b. Contents of ySet
c. Contents of both xSet and ySet
d. Intersection of contents of xSet and ySet

Ans: d

Answer Explanation:

```java
Set<String> xSet = new HashSet<String>();
xSet.add("a");
xSet.add("b");
```

```java
xSet.add("c");

Set<String> ySet = new HashSet<String>();
ySet.add("b");
ySet.add("c");
ySet.add("d");

Set zSet = new HashSet(xSet);
zSet.retainAll(ySet);

System.out.println("xSet: " + xSet);
System.out.println("ySet: " + ySet);
System.out.println("zSet: " + zSet);
```

Output:

xSet: [b, c, a]
ySet: [d, b, c]
zSet: [b, c]

In the above code zSet is initialized with contents of xSet. Call to zSet.retainAll(ySet) saves all the values that are intersection of xSet and ySet into zSet as shown in the result above.

6.7 COLLECTION ALGORITHMS

6.7.1

Which of the following functions are supported by Collections class?

static Object min(Collection elements)
static Object max(Collection elements)
static Object min(Collection elements, Comparator c)
static Object max(Collection elements, Comparator c)

static void copy(List to, List from)
static void fill(List l, Object value)
static void reverse(List l)

a. All of the above
b. None of the above
c. min and max only
d. copy, fill and reverse only

Ans: a

Answer Explanation:

max and min elements are returned according to the ordering of the elements, so all elements should implement the Comparable interface. For elements that do not implement the Comparable interface, max or min methods that use Comparator object as second parameter can be used.

In the copy() method, contents of from list is copied to the to list. In the fill() method, contents of List l is replaced by the element value. Ordering of the elements in the list are reversed using the reverse() method.

6.7.2

Following are the functions supported by Collections class

static void sort(List list)

static void sort(List list, Comparator c)

List aList = ...;
Collections.sort(aList, Collections.reverseOrder());

Running the above code snippet

a. gives compiler error
b. throws exception
c. sorts aList in reverseOrder
d. sorts aList

Ans: c

Answer Explanation:

The static method sort() of the Collections class with one List parameter should have the object in the List implement Comparable interface.

Collections.sort(List l)

The sort method can also take a second parameter if the object doesn't implement the Comparable interface. The second parameter, Comparator is used to define the ordering of the elements.

Collections.sort(List l, Comparator c)

Collections.reverseOrder() returns a Comparator that imposes the reverse ordering of the specified comparator. In the method call below, aList will get sorted in reverse order provided the objects used in aList implement the Comparable interface.

Collections.sort(aList, Collections.reverseOrder());

6.7.3

List aList = ...;
Collections.shuffle(Collections.*unmodifiableList*(aList));

The above code snippet

a. Won't compile
b. Throws UnSupportedOperationException
c. Shuffles aList elements randomly
d. Does not shuffle aList elements

Ans: b

Answer Explanation:

The shuffle() method of the Collections class shuffles the elements of a list. Since the unmodifiable list cannot be shuffled, UnSupported OperationException will be thrown.

Threads

7.1 THREAD BASICS

7.1.1

What is a thread?

1. Thread is a path of execution in a program.
2. Each thread has its own local variables, program counter, register, memory etc.
3. Threads share the same address space and therefore can share data.
4. Every process has at least one thread running within it.

Which of the above statements are true?

a. 1,3, and 4
b. 1,2, and 4
c. 1,2, and 3
d. All of the above

Ans: d

Answer Explanation:

Threads live within a process and threads share the resources within the process. A thread is a lightweight process. Threads share the address space of the process that created it, while processes have their own address space.

7.1.2

Difference between a process and a thread:

1. Threads share the address space of the process that created it, while processes have their own address space.
2. Threads can directly communicate with other threads of their process, while processes have to use inter process communication to communicate with other processes.
3. Threads can exercise considerable control over threads of the same process, while processes can execute control only over child processes.

4. Threads have direct access to data segment of the parent process, while processes have their own copy of data segment of the parent process.

Which of the above statements are false?

a. All of the above
b. None of the above
c. 1 and 2
d. 3 and 4

Ans: a

Answer Explanation:

Most JVM implementations run as a single process and each process has atleast one thread. Inter process communication which is communication between processes (within the same system or between different systems) is supported by operating systems with pipes and sockets.

In Java, Remote Method Invocation (RMI) can be used for inter process communication.

Since a process has multiple threads, a thread can be considered a lightweight process. Processes have their own set of resources like memory while threads share the memory.

7.1.3

What is a multi threaded environment?

a. An environment that allows multiple threads across multiple processes.
b. An environment that allows multiple threads to be running concurrently within a process.
c. An environment that allows both multiple threads and multiple processes concurrently.
d. None of the above

Ans: b

Answer Explanation:

Multi threading essentially means multitasking, a program that can run more than one task at a time is termed multi threaded.

A second thread other than the main thread which is always running in the Java Virtual Machine is the garbage collection thread that cleans the discarded objects and reclaims unused memory.

7.1.4

When is a class called thread-safe?

a. When the instances of a class can be safely used in a single threaded environment and no set of operations can cause it to get into an invalid state.
b. When the instances of a class can be safely used in a multi-threaded environment and no set of operations can cause it to get into an invalid state.
c. When the threads can be run safely without causing issues
d. When all methods of the class are synchronized.

Ans: b

Answer Explanation:

Fields of an object or a class should maintain a valid state when used simultaneously by multiple threads.

If a piece of code is safe to be used by multiple threads at the same time, then it's called thread-safe.

7.1.5

What are the ways to create a new class that can have a thread running within it?

a. extend the Thread class

b. implement the Runnable interface
c. extend the Thread class or implement the Runnable interface
d. extend any class

Ans: c

Answer Explanation:

For a class to be able to run a thread, it can either extend the Thread class or implement the Runnable interface and override the run() method for both.

public class ThreadDemo extends Thread {

    public void run() {

    }

}

public class RunnableDemo implements Runnable {

    public void run() {

    }

}

7.2 THREAD DEMO AND SLEEP

7.2.1

```
public class ThreadDemo extends Thread {
    public void run() {
        try {
            for(int i=0; i < 5; i++) {

                System.out.println("spawned thread");
                Thread.sleep(50);
            }
        }
        catch(InterruptedException e) {
            System.out.println("spawned thread interrupted");
        }
    }

    public static void main(String [] args) {

        ThreadDemo td = new ThreadDemo();
        td.start();

        try {
            for(int i=0; i < 5; i++) {

                System.out.println("main thread");
                Thread.sleep(50);
            }
        }
        catch(InterruptedException e) {
            System.out.println("main thread interrupted");
        }
    }
}
```

The output from running the above program is:

main thread
spawned thread
main thread

spawned thread
main thread
spawned thread
main thread
spawned thread
main thread
spawned thread

1. In a single processor machine only one thread can be run at a time.
2. The thread scheduler decides which thread runs while the other threads wait for their turn.
3. The context switching between threads happen very fast that looks like simultaneous execution.

Which of the above statements are true?

a. 1 and 2
b. 2 and 3
c. 1 and 3
d. All of the above

Ans: d

Answer Explanation:

As shown in the above program, to run a new thread, a class should extend the Thread class and override the run() method.

The main() method runs in one thread called the main thread. main() is the first method called. When a new thread is created, it runs on its own call stack separate from the stack of main.

Both these threads run independently. In a multi-processor machine, these two threads may be running at the same time, in two different processors.

In a single processor machine which is used often, thread scheduler which is part of the JVM and the operating system, work together to schedule each thread. The thread scheduler decides which thread runs while the other threads wait for their turn.

7.2.2

```java
public class ThreadDemo extends Thread {

    public void run() {
        try {
            for(int i=0; i < 5; i++) {
                System.out.println("spawned thread");
                Thread.sleep(50);
            }
        }
        catch(InterruptedException e) {
            System.out.println("spawned thread interrupted");
        }
    }

    public static void main(String [] args) {

        ThreadDemo td = new ThreadDemo();
        td.start();
        try {
            for(int i=0; i < 5; i++) {
                System.out.println("main thread");
                Thread.sleep(50);
            }
        }
        catch(InterruptedException e) {
            System.out.println("main thread interrupted");
        }
    }
}
```

The output from running the above program is:

main thread
spawned thread
main thread
spawned thread
main thread
spawned thread
main thread
spawned thread

main thread
spawned thread

The output after running the above program:

a. Is always the same
b. Depends on the thread scheduler
c. Depends on the Java VM
d. None of the above

Ans: b

Answer Explanation:

There is no guarantee that the output will be the same if the program is run again. The thread scheduler which is part of the JVM and the operating system, work together to schedule each thread. The thread scheduler decides how long each thread should be run between context switches and is dependent on the operating system.

In the above sample, ThreadDemo class extends the Thread class and overrides the run() method. In the main() method, a new ThreadDemo instance td is created. When the start method is called, this thread is ready to run and is waiting for its turn to be picked up by the thread scheduler.

Since there are two threads running, the main and the spawned thread, the thread scheduler switches between both the threads.

When multiple threads are started in a specific order, the order and duration in which they are run by the thread scheduler is not guaranteed. If the above program is run multiple times in different machines, the result will be different.

7.2.3

```
public class ThreadDemo extends Thread {
    public void run() {
        try {
            for(int i=0; i < 5; i++) {
                System.out.println("spawned thread");
                Thread.sleep(50);
            }
        }
        catch(InterruptedException e) {
            System.out.println("spawned thread interrupted");
        }
    }
    ...
}
```

In the above code, sleep method is used to

1. Stop execution of the current thread completely.
2. Suspend execution of current thread for the specified period.
3. Give a chance for other threads to run.

a. 1 and 2
b. 1 and 3
c. 2 and 3
d. All of the above

Ans. c

Answer Explanation:

sleep() method is a static method of the Thread class. It is used to suspend execution of the current thread for a specified period of time and to allow processor time for other threads to run.

When the sleep() method is called, the thread should go to sleep for at least the specified number of milliseconds in the method. If it is interrupted by another thread before the sleep time is complete, then it throws an InterruptedException.

The sleep() method can be interrupted by another thread by calling the interrupt() method.

Since the sleep() method can throw an InterruptedException, it should be used inside a try and catch block as shown in the above sample.

7.2.4

The Thread states are New, Runnable, Dead, and

a. Locked
b. Blocked
c. Stopped
d. Sleep

Answer: b

Answer Explanation:

The four main thread states are New, Runnable, Blocked, and Dead.

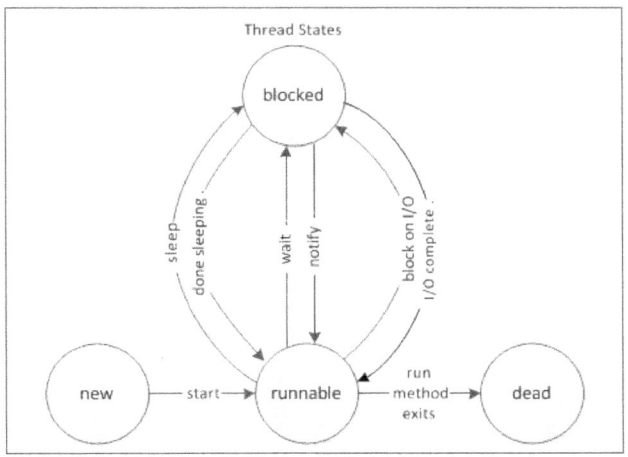

New: When a new thread is created using new and the thread is not yet running, it is in the New state.

ThreadDemo td = new ThreadDemo();

Runnable: When the start method is invoked, the thread is Runnable. A runnable thread may not be running and the scheduler will decide when to give it time to run.

td.start();

Blocked: A thread enters a blocked state when it calls the sleep(), wait() methods or when it's waiting for an I/O operation to complete or when it's trying to lock an object that is already locked by another thread.

A thread can move from blocked state to runnable state when the sleep method has completed the specified number of milliseconds, notify() or notifyAll() has been called by another thread after the wait method, I/O operation that was blocking has completed and returned, the object lock that the thread was waiting on has been relinquished by another thread holding it.

Dead: A thread dies naturally when the run() method exits normally or abruptly if the run method terminates due to an uncaught exception. stop() method can be used to kill a thread, but this method is deprecated and should not be used.

7.2.5

```
public class TimerTaskDemo extends TimerTask {

    public void run() {
        System.out.println("Timer invoked task...");
    }

    public static void main(String [] args) {

        TimerTask timerTask = new TimerTaskDemo();
        long delay = 1000;
        long period = 1000;

        Timer timer = new Timer();
        timer.schedule(timerTask, delay, period);
    }
}
```

Output:

Timer invoked task...
Timer invoked task...
Timer invoked task...
Timer invoked task...
Timer invoked task...

In the above sample, the Timer class is used to schedule

a. one time task
b. repeatable task
c. delayed one timer task
d. delayed repeatable task

Ans: d

Answer Explanation:

The Timer class can be used to schedule one time or repeatable tasks. In the above example, the Timer class is used to schedule a repeatable task in fixed intervals after a time delay before starting.

timer.schedule(timerTask, delay, period);

In the above call, timerTask is an instance of TimerTask class which implements Runnable. The task is defined inside the run() method of this class. The delay variable is the delay in milliseconds before the task is executed and the period variabe is the time in milliseconds between task executions.

7.3 RUNNABLE INTERFACE AND INTERRUPT

7.3.1

Why is it usually a good practice to implement Runnable interface rather than extend Thread class?

a. A Thread subclass cannot extend any other class as java does not support multiple inheritance.
b. Implementing the Runnable interface helps in clear separation between defining the task (Runnable interface) and executing the task (Thread class).
c. A Runnable interface represents a task and can be executed by Thread class or Executors class while Thread class has the overhead of inheriting thread management tasks.
d. All of the above.

Ans: d

Answer Explanation:

```
public class ThreadDemo extends Thread {

    public void run() {
        ------
    }

    public static void main(String [] args) {

        ThreadDemo td1 = new ThreadDemo();
        td1.start();

        ThreadDemo td2 = new ThreadDemo();
        td2.start();
    }
}

public class RunnableDemo implements Runnable {

    public void run() {
```

```
        ------
    }

    public static void main(String [] args) {

        RunnableDemo rd = new RunnableDemo();

        Thread t1 = new Thread(rd);
        t1.start();

        Thread t2 = new Thread(rd);
        t2.start();
    }
}
```

In the above sample, one object of RunnableDemo class rd is created and is shared among the threads t1 and t2. Runable interface can be used if one object needs to be shared between multiple threads.

Using ThreadDemo, two different objects td1 and td2 are created, these objects have both the thread management data as well as the state of the particular object. Same object cannot be shared between multiple threads here.

Runnable defines the task and once the task is defined it can be executed using either Thread class or java.util.concurrent.Executors class.

7.3.2

Why is it sometimes necessary to interrupt or stop a thread?

a. The thread may be executing a lengthy task.
b. The thread task may be waiting for an I/O operation or notification from another thread.
c. The thread may be sleeping for a long time.
d. All of the above.

Ans: d

Answer Explanation:

The interrupt() method is used to indicate to the thread that it should stop and do something else. If a thread is in a sleep or wait state, calling the interrupt() method breaks it out of these blocked states and throws an InterruptedException.

If the thread is not in a sleep or wait state, then the call to interrupt() method does not interrupt the thread, but sets the interrupt flag to true which can be checked using the isInterrupted() method.

7.3.3

```java
public class InterruptDemo implements Runnable {

    public void run() {
        try {
            System.out.println("spawned thread - about to sleep for
                    50 seconds");

            Thread.sleep(50000);
            System.out.println("spawned thread - done sleeping");
        }
        catch(InterruptedException e) {

            System.out.println("spawned thread - interrupted while
                    sleeping");
            return;
        }
    }

    public static void main(String [] args) {

        InterruptDemo ind = new InterruptDemo();

        Thread t = new Thread(ind);
        t.start();

        try {
            System.out.println("main thread");
            Thread.sleep(5000);
        }
```

```
            catch(InterruptedException e) {}

            System.out.println("main thread - calling interrupt");
            t. interrupt();
            System.out.println("main thread - leaving");
      }
}
```

The output on running InterruptDemo is:

main thread
spawned thread - about to sleep for 50 seconds
main thread - calling interrupt
main thread – leaving
spawned thread - interrupted while sleeping

In the above program call to t.interrupt() causes

a. the run method of the thread to throw an interrupted exception.
b. stop any operation happening in the run method and throw interrupted exception.
c. stop any operation in the run method of the thread.
d. none of the above.

Ans: b

Answer Explanation:

If a thread is in a sleep or wait state, calling the interrupt() method breaks it out of these blocked states and throws an InterruptedException.

If the thread is not in a sleep or wait state, then the call to interrupt() method does not interrupt the thread, but sets the interrupt flag to true which can be checked using the isInterrupted() method.

In the above sample, there are two threads running, the main thread and the spawned thread. The main thread is running first, and then the thread scheduler runs the spawned thread which sleeps for 50 seconds. After this, the main thread is allowed to run again when it calls the interrupt method. Finally, the spawned thread is run again which throws the InterruptedException.

7.3.4

Why are suspend, resume and stop methods deprecated?

a. These methods have been replaced by other methods.
b. There is no need to stop or suspend the thread.
c. Leads to deadlock and inconsistent state of the object.
d. None of the above.

Ans: c

Answer Explanation:

Thread.stop() can leave the objects in an inconsistent state, as calling stop method on the thread releases all the locks that the thread is holding.

Also suspend() and resume() methods can cause frequent deadlocks. If the thread that is suspended is holding a lock and another thread tries to acquire the same lock before calling the resume() method, it results in a deadlock.

7.3.5

A Daemon Thread serves other threads. When only Daemon threads are remaining, the Java virtual machine

a. continues running
b. continues or exits as needed
c. exits
d. none of the above

Ans: c

Answer Explanation:

Daemon threads are used for providing service for other threads.

If the only remaining threads in a process are daemon threads, there are no other threads to service, so the process exits.

7.3.6

```java
public class ThreadJoinDemo implements Runnable {

    public void run() {

        String threadName = Thread.currentThread().getName();

        try {
            System.out.println("Running thread: " + threadName);
            Thread.sleep(1000);
        }
        catch(InterruptedException e) {
            System.out.println(threadName + " interrupted");
        }
    }

    public static void main(String [] args) {

        String threadName = Thread.currentThread().getName();

        ThreadJoinDemo td = new ThreadJoinDemo();

        Thread t1 = new Thread(td, "t1");
        Thread t2 = new Thread(td, "t2");
        Thread t3 = new Thread(td, "t3");
        Thread t4 = new Thread(td, "t4");

        try {
            t1.start();
            t1.join();
            t2.start();
            t2.join();

            t3.start();
            t3.join();
            t4.start();
            t4.join();

            System.out.println("Running thread: " + threadName);
            Thread.sleep(1000);
        }
        catch(InterruptedException e) {
```

```
                System.out.println(threadName + " interrupted");
            }
        }
    }
```

Output:

Running thread: t1
Running thread: t2
Running thread: t3
Running thread: t4
Running thread: main

In the above program, if the join() methods for t1, t2, t3, and t4 are removed, the program output

a. order of running the threads will be the same.
b. order of running the threads will be different.
c. cannot be determined.
d. none of the above.

Ans: b

Answer Explanation:

When join() method is called on a thread instance, it blocks the currently running thread, till the thread instance which called the join method has completed executing.

In the above example, start() method followed by join() method was called for Thread instance t1. This ensures that any other running thread is stopped and t1 completes executing.

When join() method is called sequentially on the Thread objects t2, t3, and t4 as shown above, it ensures that these threads are run in the same order.

7.3.7

public class ThreadGroupDemo {

```java
public static void main(String [] args) {

    Runnable task1 = new Runnable() {

    public void run() {
        System.out.println("Executing task1");

        for(int i=0; i<1000; i++) {
            //do nothing
        }
    }
    };

    Runnable task2 = new Runnable() {

    public void run() {
        System.out.println("Executing task2'");

        for(int i=0; i<1000; i++) {
            //do nothing
        }
    }
    };

    ThreadGroup threadGroup = new
    ThreadGroup("displayGroup");

    Thread t1 = new Thread(threadGroup, task1, "t1");
    Thread t2 = new Thread(threadGroup, task2, "t2");

    t1.start();
    t2.start();

    System.out.println("name: " +
    t1.getThreadGroup().getName());

    System.out.println("activeCount: " +
    threadGroup.activeCount());
    }
}
```

Output:

name: displayGroup
activeCount: 2
Executing task1
Executing task2

ThreadGroup class shown above allows to work with

a. threads independently
b. threads as a group
c. thread dead locks
d. thread synchronization

Ans: b

Answer Explanation:

ThreadGroup class allows working with a group of threads as a single unit. It allows applying the thread primitives on thread groups. Some of the thread primitives like stop, suspend have been deprecated.

The functions that return the active count and subgroups of thread groups do not return the values accurately, so using thread groups should be avoided.

To handle a group of threads ThreadPoolExecutor class can be used.

7.3.8

```
public class ThreadPoolExecutorDemo {

    static final int CAPACITY = 5;

    int corePoolSize = 5;
    int maximumPoolSize = 5;
    long keepAliveTime = 10;

    private ThreadPoolExecutor threadPoolExecutor = null;

    private BlockingQueue<Runnable> queue =
        new LinkedBlockingQueue<Runnable>(CAPACITY);
```

```java
    public ThreadPoolExecutorDemo() {

        threadPoolExecutor =
        new ThreadPoolExecutor(corePoolSize, maximumPoolSize,
                    keepAliveTime, TimeUnit.SECONDS, queue);
    }
    public void runTask(Runnable task) {
        threadPoolExecutor.execute(task);
    }

    public void shutdown() {
        threadPoolExecutor.shutdown();
    }

    public static void main(String [] args) {

        ThreadPoolExecutorDemo tpeDemo =
            new ThreadPoolExecutorDemo();

        tpeDemo.runTask(new Runnable() {
            public void run() {
                System.out.println("Executing task1");
            }
        });

        tpeDemo.runTask(new Runnable() {
            public void run() {
                System.out.println("Executing task2");
            }
        });
    }
}
```

The above ThreadPoolExecutorDemo is an example for the following pattern

a. Strategy
b. Template Method
c. Producer Consumer
d. Observer

Ans: c

Answer Explanation:

ThreadPoolExecutor functionality shown in the above sample is an example of Producer Consumer pattern. ThreadPoolExecutor class is used to manage a pool of worker threads that are executing tasks from a work queue.

runTask() method of ThreadPoolExecutor passes the Runnable task to the execute() method.

When the execute() method is called with a new task, if the number of threads running are less than the corePoolSize, then a new thread is created to run the task. If the number of threads running are greater than the corePoolSize but less than the maximumPoolSize, the task is added to the queue.

If the queue is full, then a new thread is created. If the queue is full and the maximumPoolSize threads are busy, then the request is rejected.

In the above sample, size of corePoolSize and maximumPoolSize are both set to 5, which results in a fixed pool size.

Excess threads more than the corePoolSize which have been idle for more than the keepAliveTime will be terminated.

Using unbounded queues like LinkedBlockingQueue without predefined capacity causes any new request to be saved in the queue when all the corePoolSize threads are busy.

The number of running threads will not exceed corePoolSize, as any new request will get added to the queue. If the requests are received at a faster rate than they can be processed, then it will end in an unbounded queue growth and resource exhaustion.

This can be prevented using bounded queues like ArrayBlockingQueue which requires a predefined capacity. The queue size and the maximumPoolSize need to be tuned to handle changes in request rates. Larger queues and smaller pools minimizes CPU usage, but may not be efficient in handling increased request rates.

The choice of the queue size and the pool size should be made according to the application requirement.

7.4 THREAD PRIORITIES AND YIELD

7.4.1

Thread scheduling behavior for different thread priorities varies depending on

a. VM implementation
b. operating system
c. VM implementation and operating system
d. individual threads

Ans: c

Answer Explanation:

The scheduler in many JVMs may use time-slicing, where each thread is given a fair amount of time to run and then switched back to runnable state to give other threads a chance to run. The scheduler determines the next thread to run based on the priority and other factors. The JVM specification does not require the time-slicing scheduler to be implemented.

Some JVM schedulers may use preemptive, priority based scheduling where the highest priority thread is allowed to run till it enters a blocked state or until a higher-priority thread becomes runnable.

7.4.2

Thread.MAX_PRIORITY,Thread.NORM_PRIORITY,Thread.MIN_PRIORITY that can be passed to setPriority() method for thread scheduling priorities, have values

a. 8, 4, and 2
b. 10, 5, and 2
c. 10, 5, and 0
d. 10, 5, and 1

Ans: d

Answer Explanation:

Threads run with some priority, usually represented by a number between 1 and 10. The scheduler in most of the JVMS use time-slicing, where each thread is given a fair amount of time to run and then switched back to runnable state to give other threads a chance to run.

Thread with the highest priority is scheduled to run by the JVM. If a thread enters a runnable state and has a higher-priority than the currently running thread, then the lower-priority thread is preempted and the higher-priority thread is scheduled to run.

The default thread priority is 5. Thread class has three static final variables MAX_PRIORITY, NORM_PRIORITY and MIN_PRIORITY.

When a new thread is created, it has the same priority as the thread that created it.

7.4.3

A call to Thread.yield() relinquishes the processor to the thread-scheduler to allow another thread to run. What effect can using Thread.yield() have in terms of performance in a JVM?

a. Improved performance
b. Decreased d performance
c. No change
d. All of the above

Ans: d

Answer Explanation:

Thread.yield() may improve performance, make it worse or have no impact in a JVM.

A thread can voluntarily yield control using the yield() method. Whenever a thread yields control, it goes back to runnable state and another thread of the same priority is scheduled to run.

THREAD PRIORITIES AND YIELD

Even though yield() method takes back a thread to runnable state, it's possible that an yielding thread may be picked to run again and again by the scheduler and will not give an equal chance for all threads of the same priority to run as intended.

As a result, the performance impact of the yield method cannot be determined. Generally it is better to use sleep() method instead of yield().

7.4.4

It is better to use sleep() instead of yield() because after a call to sleep() another thread will get a chance to run, while after yield() the thread scheduler might keep reactivating the yielding thread. The above statement is

a. True
b. False

Ans: a

Answer Explanation:

A thread can voluntarily yield control using the yield() method. Whenever a thread yields control, it goes back to runnable state and another thread is scheduled to run.

Even though yield() method takes back a thread to runnable state, it's possible that a yielding thread may be picked to run again and again by the scheduler and will not give an equal chance for all threads of the same priority to run as intended.

7.4.5

ThreadLocal is used for storing

a. thread specific variables
b. local threads
c. local thread groups.

d. none of the above

Ans: a

Answer Explanation:

ThreadLocal class is used for storing thread specific variables. ThreadLocal is internally implemented using WeakHashMap that stores values associated with each thread. In the WeakHashMap, mappings that are not referenced anywhere are periodically removed by the garbage collector.

private ThreadLocal<String> threadLocalVar = **new** ThreadLocal<String>();

The ThreadLocal class supports methods initialValue(), get(), set() and remove(). The remove() method should be used to remove the thread local variables that are no longer used so that they can be removed by the garbage collector.

7.5 CONCURRENCY BASICS

7.5.1

public class StatelessDemo implements Servlet {

    public void service(ServletRequest req, ServletResponse resp) {

        System.*out*.println("Statement from Stateless!");

    }
}

Why is the above class stateless?

a. The state of the object is defined inside the class.
b. Has no fields and does not reference fields from other classes.
c. Has no fixed values that can be changed.
d. All of the above.

Ans: b

Answer Explanation:

Stateless objects are thread-safe as they have no fields and the state of the object cannot be saved.

While designing, classes should be made stateless if possible as they are thread-safe, have consistent behavior and are easy to test.

7.5.2

public class StatelessDemo implements Servlet {

    public void service(ServletRequest req, ServletResponse resp) {

        System.*out*.println("Statement from Stateless!");

        }
}

Are objects of the above stateless class thread-safe?

a. Yes, two threads accessing the stateless object do not share state and cannot affect each other.
b. No, two threads accessing the stateless object can affect each other's state.
c. Is thread-safe with two threads and not thread-safe with multiple threads.
d. None of the above.

Ans: a

Answer Explanation:

Since stateless objects have no fields, there is no object state that is shared between multiple threads, as a result stateless objects are thread-safe and less error prone.

7.5.3

public final class ImmutableDemo {

    private final Set<String> aircraftSet = new HashSet<String>();

    public ImmutableDemo() {

        aircraftSet.add("Caribou");
        aircraftSet.add("Black Hawk");
        aircraftSet.add("Spectre");
        aircraftSet.add("Goshawk");
    }

    public Set<String> getAircraftNameList() {

        return Collections.*unmodifiableSet*(aircraftSet);
    }
}

CONCURRENCY BASICS

The above class is immutable because

a. State of the object can be changed
b. The instance value is defined in the constructor
c. The class cannot be subclassed and changed
d. State of the object cannot be changed

Ans: d

Answer Explanation:

The above class ImmutableDemo is an immutable class because there are no accessor methods that can be used to change the state of the object.

aircraftSet is a mutable object, but cannot be modified using the accessor method getAircraftNameList(), which returns a unmodifiable list.

It's a good design practice to make a class immutable if possible, as immutable objects are easy to develop and test and are thread-safe.

Examples of immutable classes in java are String and Integer. To make a class immutable,

1. make the fields private and final.
2. do not provide mutator methods to modify the fields.
3. Make the class final if possible, so it cannot be subclassed.
4. If the class can be subclassed, make the methods final so they cannot be overridden.

7.5.4

public final class ImmutableDemo {

    private final Set<String> aircraftSet = new HashSet<String>();

    public ImmutableDemo() {

        aircraftSet.add("Caribou");

```
            aircraftSet.add("Black Hawk");
            aircraftSet.add("Spectre");
            aircraftSet.add("Goshawk");
        }

        public Set<String> getAircraftNameList() {

            return Collections.unmodifiableSet(aircraftSet);
        }
}
```

Are the objects of the above immutable class thread-safe?

a. Yes, as their state cannot be changed.
b. No, as their state can be changed.
c. Yes, as their state can be changed.
d. No, as their state cannot be changed.

Ans: a

Answer Explanation:

The ImmutableDemo object is immutable because the field aircraftSet cannot be changed from another class that is using it.

Using the accessor method getAircraftNameList() provided, it is not possible to change the state of the object which makes this class immutable. Immutable objects are thread-safe as there are no shared states between threads.

7.5.5

```
public class CountDemo {

    private long counter = 0;

    public long getCounter() {
        return counter;
    }

    public long incrementCounter() {
```

```
            return ++counter;
    }
}
```

Why is the above class not thread safe?

a. Because of an instance variable counter.
b. ++counter operation is not atomic.
c. ++counter operation is atomic.
d. State of the counter is not changed.

Ans: b

Answer Explanation:

The increment operation ++counter is not atomic. The incrementation is not a single indivisible operation, there are three operations involved - fetch, modify and write.

Let's say the value of counter is 10. If two threads access the incrementConter() method at the same time, after one thread has fetched the value 10, if the other thread gets a chance to run as determined by the thread scheduler, the second thread also fetches 10.

Now thread one increments the value to 11 and so does thread two. After being incremented by both the threads, the incremented value of counter will be 11 instead of 12. This is called a race condition.

thread1 – fetches 10
thread2 – fetches 10

thread2 – increments to 11
thread2 – writes 11

thread1 - increments to 11
thread1 – writes 11

Value of counter is 11, should have been 12 after being incremented by two threads.

7.5.6

What is race condition?

a. Race condition happens when the methods of a class are not synchronized.
b. Race condition happens when multiple threads are sharing state.
c. Race condition happens when two or more threads are reading or writing shared data and the final outcome is determined by how the threads are scheduled to run.
d. All of the above.

Ans: c

Answer Explanation:

Race condition happens when the state of the object gets corrupted or is set to an inconsistent state due to concurrent execution of multiple threads. Race condition happens when multiple threads operate on the same object that is not properly synchronized.

7.5.7

```
public class Singleton {

    private static Singleton instance = null;

    private Singleton() { }

    public static Singleton getInstance() {
        if(instance == null) {
            instance = new Singleton();
        }
        return instance;
    }
}
```

Above is the code snippet for lazy loading of a Singleton class, how can a race condition happen here?

a. First thread checks that instance is null and creates new Singleton object, gets swapped out, second thread checks that instance is not null and uses the already created Singleton object.
b. First thread checks that instance is null and gets swapped out, second thread also checks that instance is null and both the threads create a new Singleton object.
c. All threads share state of the Singleton object which is the instance variable 'instance'.
d. All of the above.

Ans: b

Answer Explanation:

Let's assume that the above program is run in a multi-threaded environment and two threads are accessing the getInstance() method simultaneously.

Thread1 accesses the getInstance() method and executes till the check for null instance

if(*instance* == null)

and then gets swapped out. Thread2 accesses and creates a new Singleton object and returns it. When thread1 is allowed to run again, it also creates a new Singleton instance as the check for null instance was made already.

This results in a race condition, the two threads returning two different instances of the Singleton class which is not according to the intended design.

7.5.8

public class VolatileDemo implements Runnable {

    private volatile boolean ready;

    public VolatileDemo() {

        ready = false;

```
    }
    public void run() {

        while(ready) {
            //do something
        }
    }

    public void readyNow() {

        ready = true;
    }

    public static void main(String[] args) {

        VolatileDemo volDemo = new VolatileDemo();

        Thread t = new Thread(volDemo);
        t.start();

        volDemo.readyNow();
        System.out.println("Just set ready to true");
    }
}
```

In the VolatileDemo class, instance variable ready is made volatile because

a. the variable is being read and written by the same thread.
b. the variable is being set by one thread and checked by another thread and should reflect the latest value.
c. the variable is being set by one thread and checked by another thread and should be atomic.
d. all of the above.

Ans: b

Answer Explanation:

The volatile keyword ensures that the value is read from the main memory and not from the thread's local cache. Write changes of individual threads are also saved to the main memory.

Without the use of volatile variable, the compiler is free to reorder code and cache the values instead of reading from the main memory.

In the above sample, the volatile variable ready is being set to true from the main thread by calling the readyNow() method. The second thread checks this value inside the run() method. Read and write operations on this volatile variable are being performed from two different threads.

This volatile variable value is always accessed from the main memory and updated to the main memory as a result of which, the most recent value will be accessible from all the threads.

7.5.9

Volatile variables can guarantee visibility but not

a. synchronization
b. mutual exclusion
c. locking
d. atomicity

Ans: d

Answer Explanation:

Volatile variables are modifiers used on member variables to indicate that the variable should be read from main memory when accessed from individual threads. Also the individual threads should save the write changes to the main memory.

When a volatile variable is used, two different threads will always see the most recent value of the member variable from the shared memory and not any local cached values.

Volatile variables do not support atomicity. If an increment operator is used on a volatile variable, the read, increment and write operations are not atomic as a result of which volatile variables cannot be used in counters.

7.6 CONCURRENCY AND SYNCHRONIZATION

7.6.1

```java
public class CountDemo {

    private int counter = 0;

    public synchronized int getCounter() {

        return counter;
    }
    public synchronized int incrementCounter() {

        return ++counter;
    }
}
```

Is the above CountDemo class thread safe?

a. Yes
b. No

Ans: a

Answer Explanation:

The synchronized method for an object can be accessed by only one thread at a time. If more threads try to execute synchronized methods on the same object, they will be blocked till the first thread completes executing the method.

This is possible because once the first thread enters the synchronized method, it holds an object lock till it completes the method execution. Once done, it relinquishes the lock and one of the blocked threads will be picked by the thread scheduler to acquire the lock and execute the method.

Synchronization ensures that multiple threads cannot modify a shared object simultaneously thus preventing the object from being corrupted.

CONCURRENCY AND SYNCHRONIZATION

7.6.2

```
public class CountDemo {

    private int counter = 0;

    public synchronized int getCounter() {

        return counter;
    }
    public synchronized int incrementCounter() {

        return ++counter;
    }
}
```

How does the above code snippet guarantee visibility and atomicity of the state variable, counter among different threads?

a. Because of synchronized modifier, only one thread is allowed inside the method at a time and this keeps out other threads from changing the state of the object at the same time.
b. When a thread calls a synchronized method, the object becomes locked and other threads cannot execute the synchronized method.
c. When a thread calls a synchronized method, it is guaranteed that the method will finish execution before another thread can execute any synchronized method on the same object.
d. All of the above

Ans: d

Answer Explanation:

If one thread is executing synchronized method on an object, this thread owns an object lock and any other thread that tries to execute any synchronized method on the same object is blocked.

It's guaranteed that a thread accessing a synchronized method can complete fully before any other thread is granted access to execute the same method. This ensures visibility and atomicity.

In the above sample if one thread on an object calls the incrementCounter() method, all other threads will be blocked to execute any synchronized method on this object, till this method execution is complete.

Incrementing the integer is not an atomic operation and involves fetch, add and write. When the thread enters the synchronized method incrementCounter(), it acquires the lock, reads the value from the main memory, performs the increment operation, writes to the main memory and releases the lock.

When this thread is holding the lock and executing the method, no other thread is allowed to execute any synchronized method on the same object.

Once the incrementation is done, if the next thread that is granted access, calls the getCounter() method which is also synchronized, the updated value of the counter will be fetched. Visibility and atomicity are thus ensured using these synchronized methods.

7.6.3

public class ThreadObjectDemo {

    private String name;

    ThreadObjectDemo(String objectName) {

        this.name = objectName;
    }

    public synchronized void printName() {

        String tName = Thread.*currentThread*().getName();

        System.*out*.println(tName + ": " + name+ ": entering printName()");

        try {
            System.*out*.println(tName + ": " + name + ": ....about to sleep");

            Thread.*sleep*(3000);

```java
        }
        catch(InterruptedException ie) {
            System.out.println(" Interrupted");
        }

        System.out.println(tName + ": " + name+ ": leaving
        printName()");
    }

    public static void main(String [] args) {

        //create two new objects
        final ThreadObjectDemo objectA =
            new ThreadAndObject("objectA");

        final ThreadObjectDemo objectB =
            new ThreadAndObject("objectB");

        //create two new threads
        Runnable run1 = new Runnable() {

            public void run() {
                objectA.printName();
            }
        };

        Thread t1 = new Thread(run1, "thread1");
        t1.start();

        Runnable run2 = new Runnable() {

            public void run() {
                objectB.printName();
            }
        };

        Thread t2 = new Thread(run2, "thread2");
        t2.start();
    }
}
```

Output:

thread1: objectA: entering printName()
thread1: objectA: ....about to sleep

thread2: objectB: entering printName()
thread2: objectB: ....about to sleep

thread1: objectA: leaving printName()
thread2: objectB: leaving printName()

Above is the code snippet and output with two objects and two threads. Can two different threads execute on a synchronized method of two different objects simultaneously?

a. Yes
b. No

Ans: a

Answer Explanation:

In the main() method of the above sample, two new objects, objectA and objectB are created. Then thread1 is created which invokes the printName() method on objectA, and thread2 the same method on objectB.

When both the threads are run, as shown in the output, thread1 invokes the printName() method on objectA, after this it sleeps and thread2 comes alive and also executes printName() and then goes to sleep. After this, thread1 wakes up and completes executing the method followed by thread2.

From the output it's clear that the synchronized method printName() is accessed by thread2 before thread1 completes. This is possible because both the threads are holding locks on different objects, thread1 for objectA and thread2 for objectB.

If both the threads were operating on the same object, then the second thread will not be allowed to execute the synchronized method till the first thread completes execution as shown in the output below.

If the above sample is modified so that thread2 also runs objectA.printName(), then the output will be:

thread1: objectA: entering printName()
thread1: objectA: ....about to sleep
thread1: objectA: leaving printName()

thread2: objectA: entering printName()
thread2: objectA: ....about to sleep
thread2: objectA: leaving printName()

Thread2 enters the printName() method only after thread1 has completed executing this synchronized method as thread1 has to relinquish the object lock before thread2 can start executing this method.

7.6.4

code snippet1:

```
public synchronized long getCounter() {

    return counter;
}
```

code snippet2:

```
public long getCounter() {

    synchronized(this) {
        return counter;
    }
}
```

a. The two codes exactly do the same thing.
b. They are both different in functionality.
c. First one synchronizes the method and the next acquires exclusive access to object-level lock.
d. None of the above.

Ans: a

Answer Explanation:

In the above sample, both the synchronized method and the synchronized block acquire the lock on the object which is operating on the method. When synchronized method is used, the lock is acquired on the current instance. While using the synchronized block also, lock is acquired on the current instance 'this' and portions of the code that need not be synchronized can be moved out of the block.

7.6.5

```
public void setPoints(int a, int b) {
    ------
    ------
    synchronized(this) {
        this.x = a;
        this.y = b;
    }
}
```

In the above code snippet, why is synchronized block used instead of making the method synchronized?

a. Synchronized block is used to reduce the time that the object-level lock is held.
b. Synchronized block gives granular control over the lock.
c. Synchronized block improves performance by excluding portions of code that need not be locked.
d. All of the above.

Ans: d

Answer Explanation:

Specific portions of the code can be synchronized using synchronized block instead of synchronizing the whole method. This improves performance since lock is held on smaller portions for shorter period of time.

While using the synchronized block, a lock can be acquired on any object (not just this object) and also portions of the code that need not be synchronized can be moved out of the block.

7.6.6

```
synchronized(mutex) {
    ------
    ------
}
```

In the above code snippet, mutex refers to

a. this object
b. any object
c. locked object
d. all of the above

Ans: b

Answer Explanation:

Using a synchronized block, a lock can be acquired on any object. If the synchronized block is inside a static method, it can acquire a class level lock.

A synchronized method can be replaced with a synchronized block with lock on the current object 'this'. Synchronized block has the flexibility of acquiring the lock on any object not just the current object.

```
public Object lock1 = new Object();

public void methodA() {

    synchronized (lock1) {
        //do something
    }
}
```

7.6.7

When the thread leaves the synchronized block, it automatically releases the lock. Which of the following actions within the block indicate that the thread is leaving?

a. return statement, throw statement
b. calling another method
c. sleep
d. all of the above

Ans: a

Answer Explanation:

Before entering the synchronized block, the thread acquires the lock, reads the data from the main memory. When it leaves the block, writes the data back to the main memory and releases the lock. The return statement or throw statement within the synchronization block can force it to exit the block, thus releasing the lock.

7.6.8

```
public class StaticCounter1 {

    private static int counter = 0;
    ------
    ------
    public static synchronized void incrementCounter() {

        ++counter;
    }
}
public class StaticCounter2 {

    private static int counter = 0;
    ------
    ------
    public static void incrementCounter() {

        synchronized(StaticCounter2.class) {

            ++counter;
        }
    }
}
```

a. incrementCounter method in StaticCounter1 is valid but same method in StaticCounter2 is not valid.
b. incrementCounter method in StaticCounter2 is valid but same method in StaticCounter1 is not valid.
c. incrementCounter method in both the classes are valid and have same functionality.
d. none of the above.

Ans: c

Answer Explanation:

When a static method is synchronized, the class level lock is acquired. The thread executing the static synchronized method, acquires a class level lock during method execution.

Similarly when a synchronization block is used inside a static method, a class level lock can be used as shown in the above sample. Synchronization using a class level lock ensures that only one thread can execute the code on one instance of the class at any point of time.

7.6.9

Why are methods of the Collections API not synchronized by default?

a. Synchronization is not needed by default for most of the operations.
b. Acquiring and releasing lock every time reduces performance.
c. All of the above.
d. None of the above.

Ans: c

Answer Explanation:

Synchronization involves performance costs in handling locks and threads and should be used only if necessary. Collections API methods are not synchronized by default as most operations usually don't require synchronization.

Collections.synchronizedCollection() method can be used to synchronize a collection.

7.7 DEADLOCKS, WAIT AND NOTIFY

7.7.1

Thread1 is holding lock1 and is trying to acquire lock2. Meanwhile, Thread2 is holding lock2 and trying to acquire lock1 which is already being held by thread1. If both thread1 and thread2 are endlessly waiting for each other to release the lock, it is called

a. deadlock
b. race condition
c. synchronization
d. mutex

Ans: a

Answer Explanation:

Deadlock happens when two or more threads are blocked and are waiting forever for each other to release the lock.

In the above scenario described, both Thread1 and Thread2 are waiting for each other to release the lock which results in a deadlock.

7.7.2

For avoiding deadlocks, the following method can help

a. Hold locks for minimal amount of time by using synchronized statement blocks instead of synchronized methods.
b. Do not hold more than one lock at a time, if that's not possible make the second lock to be held for a short period of time.
c. Instead of multiple object-level locks, just one large lock can be used.
d. all of the above.

Ans: d

Answer Explanation:

Deadlock happens usually when there are multiple object locks held in different orders as shown below.

public static Object lock1 = **new** Object();

public static Object lock2 = **new** Object();

public void methodA() {

    synchronized (lock1) {
        synchronized (lock2) {
            //do something
        }
    }
}

public void methodB() {

    synchronized (lock2) {
        synchronized (lock1) {
            //do something
        }
    }
}

In the above sample, deadlock happens if thread1 calls methodA() and thread2 calls methodB() at the same time. methodA() acquires lock1 and tries to acquire lock2, meanwhile methodB() has already acquired lock2 and tries to acquire lock1 which is already being held. This results in a deadlock.

This deadlock can be avoided by changing the code so that more than one lock is not held at a time. If it's necessary to hold more than one lock at a time, then the locks accessed from different methods can be held in the same order.

If the locks are held in the same order in both the methods, then it would not result in a deadlock.

Making lock1 and lock2 as static variables simplifies the above locking mechanism as there can be only one instance of lock1 and lock2 for all instances of the class.

7.7.3

```java
public class DeadlockDemo {

    private String name;

    DeadlockDemo(String objectName) {
        this.name = objectName;
    }
    public String getName() {
        return name;
    }

    public synchronized void method1(DeadlockDemo dlObject) {

        String tName = Thread.currentThread().getName();
        System.out.println(tName+": "+name+": entering method1()");

        try {
            System.out.println(tName+": "+name+".... about to sleep");
            Thread.sleep(1000);

            System.out.println(tName+": "+name+" call method2 of "+dlObject.getName());
            dlObject.method2();
        }
        catch(InterruptedException ie) {
            System.out.println("method1 Interrupted");
        }
        System.out.println(tName + ": "+name+": leaving method1()");
    }
    public synchronized void method2() {

        String threadName = Thread.currentThread().getName();
        System.out.println(threadName+": "+name+": entering method2()");

        try {
            System.out.println(threadName+": "+name);
            Thread.sleep(1000);
```

```java
        }
        catch(InterruptedException ie) {
            System.out.println("method2 Interrupted");
        }
        System.out.println(threadName+": "+name+": leaving
        method2()");
    }

    public static void main(String [] args) {

        final DeadlockDemo objectA =
            new DeadlockDemo("objectA");

        final DeadlockDemo objectB =
            new DeadlockDemo("objectB");

        Runnable run1 = new Runnable() {
            public void run() {
                objectA.method1(objectB);
            }
        };
        Thread thread1 = new Thread(run1, "thread1");
        thread1.start();

        Runnable run2 = new Runnable() {
            public void run() {
                objectB.method1(objectA);
            }
        };
        Thread thread2 = new Thread(run2, "thread2");
        thread2.start();

        try {
            Thread.sleep(2000);
            System.out.println("before calling thread1 interrupt");
            thread1.interrupt();

            Thread.sleep(1000);
            System.out.println("before calling thread2 interrupt");
            thread2.interrupt();
        }
        catch(InterruptedException ie) {
            System.out.println("Interrupted");
```

            }
        }
}

Output:

thread1: objectA: entering method1()
thread1: objectA.... about to sleep

thread2: objectB: entering method1()
thread2: objectB.... about to sleep

thread1: objectA call method2 of objectB
thread2: objectB call method2 of objectA

before calling thread1 interrupt
before calling thread2 interrupt

In the above program, did the call to thread1 and thread2 interrupt remove the deadlock situation?

a. Yes
b. No

Ans: b

Answer Explanation:

In the above sample, thread1 invokes objectA.method1() and thread2 invokes objectB.method1()

objectA passes objectB as the method1 parameter and objectB passes objectA as the method1 parameter.

Since method1() is synchronized, inside this method, thread1 is holding a lock to objectA and thread2 is holding a lock to objectB and they are running concurrently as seen in the output.

Since thread1 and thread2 are operating on two different objects, once thread1 goes to sleep thread2 is invoked to run the method1() after which thread2 also goes to sleep.

DEADLOCKS, WAIT AND NOTIFY

At this instance, thread1 is inside method1() and has lock on objectA, and thread2 is also inside method1() with an lock on objectB. After this, thread1 wakes up and tries to acquire lock on objectB (to execute method2()) which is being held by thread2, so thread1 waits.

Similarly, thread2 wakes up and tries to acquire lock on objectA which is held by thread1 and waits. Thread1 and thread2 are waiting for each other simultaneously and this results in a deadlock.

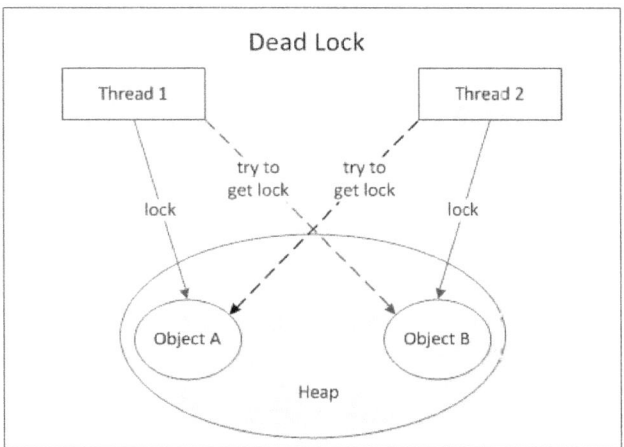

Interrupt does not unblock the threads that are deadlocked. There is no reliable method to unblock deadlocked threads and return objects in a consistent state, the code should be examined and designed to avoid deadlocks.

7.7.4

public class Queue {

    private int maxCapacity;
    private int [] queArray;
    private int rear;
    private int front;

```java
private int nItems;

public Queue(int cap) {

    maxCapacity = (cap > 0)? cap:1;
    queArray = new int[maxCapacity];
    rear = 0;
    front = 0;
    nItems = 0;
}

public synchronized boolean isFull() {

    return nItems == maxCapacity;
}

public synchronized boolean isEmpty() {

    return nItems == 0;
}

public synchronized void add(int i) throws InterruptedException {

    while (isFull()) {
        wait();
    }
    queArray[rear] = i;
    rear = (rear+1) % maxCapacity;

    nItems++;
    notifyAll();
}

public synchronized int remove() throws InterruptedException{

    int temp = -1;
    while (isEmpty()) {
        wait();
    }
    temp = queArray[front];

    queArray[front] = -1;
    front =(front+1)%maxCapacity;
```

```
            nItems--;
            notifyAll();

            return temp;
        }
}
```

In the above program, if remove() is called and isEmpty() returns true, sequence of steps that follow are

1. The thread calls wait and is put in the wait list.
2. When another thread executes add and calls notifyAll() on the same object, the waiting thread is removed from the wait list.
3. The active threads will try to re enter the object, and once the specific thread acquires the object lock, it executes the rest of the remove() code.

a. 1 and 2
b. 2 and 3
c. None of the above
d. All of the above

Ans: d

Answer Explanation:

When wait() method is called inside a synchronized method, the thread enters a blocked state and relinquishes the lock. This allows another thread to change the object state.

When the wait() method is called, the thread enters a blocked state and becomes runnable only if notify() or notifyAll() method is called by another thread. Once the thread is runnable, the scheduler will activate it.

The notify() method moves one arbitrary thread that has called wait() from blocked to runnable state, while notifyAll() method removes all threads out of blocked state to runnable state.

The above sample is an implementation of a FIFO queue using an integer array. In the add() method, if isFull() check is true then the wait() method is called and the thread goes to wait state.

If another thread invokes the remove() method, it removes the item in the front of the list and calls notifyAll() method. The waiting thread is now unblocked and is runnable, which will be eventually picked by the thread scheduler to run.

When this thread is picked to run again, it adds the value to the end of the list and calls notifyAll() again to unblock any other waiting threads.

7.7.5

Why is it recommended to use notify() instead of notifyAll()?

a. It's possible that notify may invoke the wrong thread.
b. It's possible that notify invokes the same thread again and again.
c. notify() removes only one thread from the wait list while notifyAll() removes all threads from the wait list, so all the threads get a chance to run again which is safer.
d. All of the above.

Ans: d

Answer Explanation:

When the wait() method is called, the thread enters a blocked state and becomes runnable only if notify() or notifyAll() method is called by another thread. The notify() method unblocks one arbitrary waiting thread, while notifyAll() method removes all threads out of blocked state to runnable state.

If the thread that is unblocked by the notify() method is the wrong thread, then the other waiting threads can end up waiting endlessly which can result in a deadlock situation. It's recommended to use notifyAll() so that all the waiting threads get unblocked.

7.7.6

Both sleep() and wait() methods take the current thread into non runnable state

a. with sleep() method, the current thread still owns the lock, while with wait() method it releases the lock.
b. with sleep() method, the current thread releases the lock, while with wait() method it still owns the lock.
c. and both methods belong to the Thread class.
d. None of the above.

Ans: a

Answer Explanation:

Thread.sleep() sleeps till the time specified has elapsed. Sleep sends the current thread into a non runnable state for the specified period of time, but the thread still owns the lock for the object.

If the sleep() method is executing inside a synchronized method, then no other thread of the same object will be able to enter the method.

Object.wait() waits till notify() or notifyAll() is called by another thread. The wait() method also sends the current thread to non runnable state, but the locks are released before going to the non runnable state.

7.7.7

```java
public class QueueWaitOutsideLoop {

    int [] arr;
    int maxCapacity=0;

    int front=0;
    int rear=0;
    int nItems=0;

    public QueueWaitOutsideLoop(int size) {

        maxCapacity = size;
        arr = new int [maxCapacity];
    }
```

```java
public synchronized boolean isEmpty() {
    return nItems == 0;
}

public synchronized boolean isFull() {
    return nItems == maxCapacity;
}

public synchronized void add(int n) throws InterruptedException {

    if(isFull()) {
        wait();
    }

    arr[rear] = n;
    rear = (rear+1) % maxCapacity;
    nItems++;

    System.out.println(Thread.currentThread().getName()    +   "
    :printQueue after add");
    printQueue();

    notifyAll();

}

public synchronized int remove() throws InterruptedException {

    int temp = -1;

    if(isEmpty()) {
        wait();
    }
    temp = arr[front];

    arr[front] = -1;
    front = (front+1) % maxCapacity;
    nItems--;

    System.out.println(Thread.currentThread().getName()    +   "
    :printQueue after remove");
```

```java
        printQueue();

        notifyAll();

        return temp;
    }

    public void printQueue() {

        System.out.println(Arrays.toString(arr) + " front: " + front + " rear: " + rear);

        System.out.println("nItems: " + nItems + "\n");
    }


    public static void main(String [] args) {

        System.out.println("QueueWaitOutsideLoop \n");

        QueueWaitOutsideLoop q = new QueueWaitOutsideLoop(2);

        //thread1
        Runnable run1 = new Runnable() {
            public void run() {

                try {
                    q.remove();
                }
                catch(InterruptedException ie) {

                    System.out.println("InterruptedException");
                }

            }
        };

        Thread thread1 = new Thread(run1, "thread1");
        thread1.start();
```

```java
//thread2
Runnable run2 = new Runnable() {
    public void run() {

        try {
            q.remove();
        }
        catch(InterruptedException ie) {

            System.out.println("InterruptedException");
        }

    }
};

Thread thread2 = new Thread(run2, "thread2");
thread2.start();

//thread3
Runnable run3 = new Runnable() {
    public void run() {

        try {
            q.add(1);
        }
        catch(InterruptedException ie) {

            System.out.println("InterruptedException");
        }

    }
};

Thread thread3 = new Thread(run3, "thread3");
thread3.start();

//thread4
Runnable run4 = new Runnable() {
    public void run() {

        try {
```

```
                    q.add(2);
                }
                catch(InterruptedException ie) {
                    System.out.println("InterruptedException");
                }
            }
        };

        Thread thread4 = new Thread(run4, "thread4");
        thread4.start();
    }
}
```

Output:

QueueWaitOutsideLoop

thread3 :printQueue after add
[1, 0] front: 0 rear: 1
nItems: 1

thread1 :printQueue after remove
[-1, 0] front: 1 rear: 1
nItems: 0

thread2 :printQueue after remove
[-1, -1] front: 0 rear: 1
nItems: -1

thread4 :printQueue after add
[-1, 2] front: 0 rear: 0
nItems: 0

Why Object.wait() method should not be invoked outside a loop?

a. Without the loop, wait() method invoked can cause the thread to wait endlessly.
b. If wait is called outside the loop without check on state of the variable, the condition may not be valid after the thread acquires the lock.

c. If wait() method is called outside the loop it may be invoked too many times unnecessarily.
d. All of the above.

Ans: b

Answer Explanation:

The above sample is an implementation of a FIFO queue using an integer array. Thread1 starts first and in the remove() method, checks if the queue is empty using isEmpty() method. Since the queue is empty, the thread calls wait and goes to the wait state.

Next Thread2 is started and this thread also, in the remove() method, goes to the wait state after checking that the queue is empty.

Thread3 is started next and the add() method is invoked. In the add() method, isFull() check is not true, so the integer 1 passed is added to the queue. At the end of the add method, notifyAll() method is called to unblock the waiting threads.

The waiting threads Thread1 and Thread2 are unblocked and are in runnable state now. Thread1 and Thread2 get chance to run again one after the other for a short interval of time as picked by the thread scheduler. Thread1 and Thread2 inside the remove() method call the isEmpty() method one after the other. Since the queue is not empty, Thread1 and Thread2 attempt to remove the item in the Queue one after the other. This leaves the Queue object in an inconsistent state.

When the if statements in the add() and remove() methods are replaced by while loop, then the output of the above sample will be:

Output:

thread3 :printQueue after add
[1, 0] front: 0 rear: 1
nItems: 1

thread1 :printQueue after remove
[-1, 0] front: 1 rear: 1
nItems: 0

thread4 :printQueue after add

[-1, 2] front: 1 rear: 0
nItems: 1

thread2 :printQueue after remove
[-1, -1] front: 0 rear: 0
nItems: 0

After adding the while loop, in the remove method, isEmpty() check is inside a while loop. After the Thread1 removes the item, when Thread2 is invoked, Thread2 checks inside the while loop if the Queue is empty. Since the Queue is empty, calls wait() and goes to the wait state.

After Thread4 adds an item and invokes the notifyAll() method, then thread2 wakes up and checks that the Queue is not Empty and removes the item from the Queue.

When each thread acquires the lock, since the validity of the condition is checked inside a loop, the object state is determined correctly before the next action is performed. This way, the consistent state of the object is maintained.

JDBC

8.1 JDBC BASICS

8.1.1

In a three-tier architecture, JDBC (Java Database Connectivity) is used to manage communication between

a. client and backend database
b. middle tier and backend database
c. client and middle tier
d. none of the above

Ans: b

Answer Explanation:

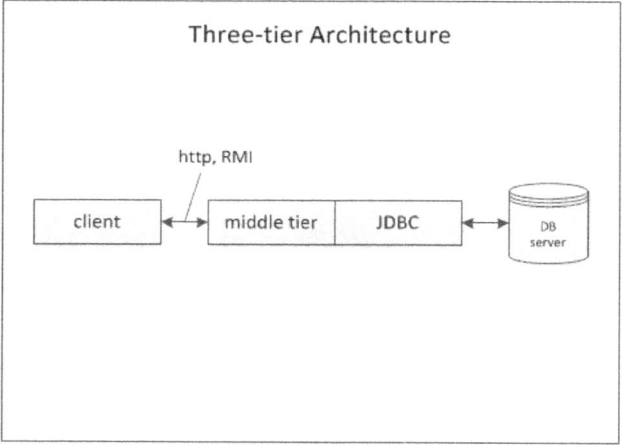

The three-tier model has a client that is the presentation layer, middle tier that is the business logic layer and the database which is the data layer. HTTP, RMI or other protocols can be used for communication between the client and middle tier while communication between middle tier and database can happen using JDBC.

JDBC BASICS

8.1.2

JDBC API communicates with JDBC driver manager, while JDBC driver manager talks to the database using drivers provided by

a. JDBC vendors
b. database vendors
c. JDBC
d. database

Ans: b

Answer Explanation:

Each database vendor provide drivers that are used by the JDBC driver manager to communicate with the underlying database like mysql, postgres, oracle, mongodb, dynamodb, couchbase etc.

8.1.3

Context jndiContext = new InitialContext();

DataSource dataSource = (DataSource) jndiContext.lookup("...");

Connection conn = dataSource.getConnection();

The above code snippet is used for opening a database connection using

a. Java Naming and Directory interface
b. Connection Pooling
c. Property file
d. Distributed transactions

Ans: a

Answer Explanation:

Database connection management can be integrated with Java Naming and Directory interface. The directory manages the location of the data sources. In the above code, the jndi service locates the data source. The Datasource object is a representation of a data source that is used for storing data which could be a database or a file.

8.1.4

The DataSource object represents a data source which is a

a. data storage unit
b. complex database
c. file in a remote server
d. all of the above

Ans: d

Answer Explanation:

The Datasource object is a representation of a data source that is used for storing data which could be a database or a file.

8.2 STATEMENT, QUERY AND TRANSACTIONS

8.2.1

```
Statement stmt = con.createStatement();

String command = "UPDATE Product "
 + "SET Price = Price - 2.00 "
 + "WHERE Name LIKE '%News%'";

int rowCount = stmt.executeUpdate(command);
```

In the above code snippet, 'command' can also specify following actions

a. CREATE TABLE, DROP TABLE
b. INSERT, UPDATE, DELETE
c. All of the above
d. None of the above

Ans: c

Answer Explanation:

The command for executeUpdate() method can be actions like INSERT, UPDATE, DELETE, CREATE TABLE and DROP TABLE. The executeUpdate() method returns the number of rows that were affected by the operation.

8.2.2

```
try {
    con.setAutoCommit(false);

    Statement stmt = con.createStatement();

    stmt.executeUpdate(command1);
    stmt.executeUpdate(command2);
    stmt.executeUpdate(command3);
```

```
        con.commit();
}
catch(SQLException e) {

        con.rollback();
        throw e;
}
```

In the above code snippet, con.setAutoCommit(false) and con.commit() are used to group the commands into transactions to ensure

a. transaction integrity
b. database integrity
c. group command execution
d. all of the above

Ans: b

Answer Explanation:

The commands are grouped into transactions for database integrity. When the commands are grouped into a transaction, if all the updates succeed then the transaction has succeeded and can be committed. If any of the update fails, then the transaction can be rolled back. Rollback will undo all the updates since the last commit and thus maintains the state of the database in an error scenario.

A transaction is a set of commands that are executed as a single unit. All the commands succeed or fail as a single unit. Even if a single command fails, all the commands are rolled back and the database is restored back to the state it was before starting the command execution. This ensures database integrity.

8.2.3

If an error occurred during a transaction, to undo any changes since the last commit, the following command can be used

a. con.uncommit()
b. con.undo()
c. con.rollback()

d. all of the above

Ans: c

Answer Explanation:

rollback() method is usually called when the transaction throws a SQLException. Rollback will undo all the changes since the last commit. By default, database connection is in autocommit mode and each SQL command is committed to the database as soon as it's executed.

Once a command is committed, it cannot be rolled back. To execute a set of commands in a single transaction so they succeed or fail as a single unit, setAutoCommit() can be set to false at the beginning of the transaction as follows

```
try {
    con.setAutoCommit(false);

    Statement stmt = con.createStatement();
    stmt.executeUpdate(command1);
    stmt.executeUpdate(command2);
    stmt.executeUpdate(command3);

    con.commit();
}
catch(SQLException e) {
    con.rollback();
    throw e;
}
```

8.2.4

```
ResultSet rs = stmt.executeQuery("SELECT * FROM Product");

while(rs.next()) {

    String name = rs.getString(1);
    float price = rs.getDouble("Price");
    ------
}
```

In the above code snippet for query execution, 1 and "Price" refer to

a. column number and column name
b. row number and row name
c. entity number and entity name
d. None of the above

Ans: a

Answer Explanation:

rs.getString(1) takes the numeric argument and returns the value of the first column in the current row. This argument refers to the column number.

rs.getDouble("Price") takes the String argument and returns the value of the column with name "Price". This argument refers to the column name. The numeric argument is more efficient, but the string arguments can be used for easy code readability and maintainability.

8.2.5

Difference between Statement and PreparedStatement

a. PreparedStatement is compiled only once in the database side and can be used multiple times after that, while Statement is compiled on the database side every time it is executed.
b. PreparedStatement can be used if large number of identical queries are used with different values. Statements are good for one time insert and updates.
c. Statements are also good for batch inserts or updates.
d. All of the above

Ans: d

Answer Explanation:

String command =
"insert into Product (Name) values (?) where id = ?";

```
PreparedStatement pstmt = conn.prepareStatement(command);
while (...) //terminating loop
{
    pstmt.setString(strVar);
    pstmt.setInt(intVar);
    pstmt.execute();
}
```

conn.preparedStatement() makes a call to the database to precompile the sql string, then another call is made to the database when pstmt.execute() is called. When the number of iterations is large, PreparedStatement is twice as fast as Statement. Statements are good for one time insert or update.

```
Statement stmt = con.createStatement();
String command = "UPDATE Product "
+ "SET Price = Price - 2.00 "
+ "WHERE Name LIKE '%News%'";
int rowCount = stmt.executeUpdate(command);
```

Statements are also good for batch operations as shown below.

```
String cmd1 = "insert into Product ...";
String cmd2 = "update Product ...";
Statement st = conn.createStatement();
st.addBatch(cmd1);
st.addBatch(cmd2);
int[] rows = st.executeBatch();
```

PreparedStatements are best used while executing a large number of identical queries with different values. PreparedStatement can be used while looping through the code when rows are added and updated in bulk, otherwise Statement can be used.

Statements are good for one time inserts and updates. Statements are also good for sending in several different batches of inserts and updates.

Design Patterns

9.1 CREATIONAL PATTERNS

9.1.1

public class Singleton {

    private static Singleton instance = new Singleton();

    private Singleton() { }

    public static Singleton getInstance() { return instance; }
}

The above Singleton class ensures

a. no instance
b. one instance
c. two instances
d. multiple instances

Ans: b

Answer Explanation:

Singleton is a creational pattern and ensures that there is only single instance of the class. This is achieved by making the constructor private and providing a static accessor method for the instance which in the above example is called getInstance().

The above implementation of singleton is simple, but creates the instance even before getInstance() method is called for the first time. This is not a good design if the singleton object is not always used and takes up lots of resources. In this kind of scenario, lazy-loading should be used and the class creation should happen after getInstance() is called for the first time.

9.1.2

public class Singleton2 {

CREATIONAL PATTERNS

```
        private static Singleton2 instance = null;

        private Singleton2() { }

        public static Singleton2 getInstance() {
            if(instance == null) {
                instance = new Singleton2();
            }
            return instance;
        }

        public static void main(String [] args) {
            Singleton2.getInstance();
        }
}
```

Will the above implementation of Singleton pattern using lazy initialization work well for a multi-threaded environment?

a. Yes
b. No

Ans: b

Answer Explanation:

Singleton2 has the implementation for lazy initialization where a new instance is created after getInstance() is called for the first time.

Inside getInstance() the check for instance == null, ensures that the instance is created only for the first time and returns the created instance in the subsequent calls.

In a multi-threaded environment, if two threads access the getInstance() method at the same time, it's possible that both threads detect instance as null and both create a new Singleton2 instance, resulting in two different instances returned. To prevent this, getInstance() method should be synchronized.

9.1.3

```
public class Singleton3 {

    private Singleton3() {}

    private static class SingletonHolder {

        static Singleton3 instance = new Singleton3();
    }

    public static Singleton3 getInstance() {

        return SingletonHolder.instance;
    }

    public static void main(String [] args) {

        Singleton3 single = Singleton3.getInstance();
    }
}
```

Will the above implementation of Singleton pattern using static inner class work for multi-threaded environment?

a. Yes
b. No

Ans: a

Answer Explanation:

The above implementation of Singleton using static inner class for lazy loading is a good solution for multi-threaded environment.

In the Singleton3 class, getInstance() method calls static variable instance, of private static inner class SingletonHolder which instantiates and returns the Singleton3 instance for the first time and the already created instance during subsequent calls and is safe in a multi-threaded environment.

9.1.4

```
public interface Fruit {
    void pick();
}

public class Strawberry implements Fruit {

    public void pick() {System.out.println("Pick a strawberry");}
}

public class Banana implements Fruit {

    public void pick() {System.out.println("Pick a banana");}
}

public class FruitFactory {

    public static Fruit getFruit(String fruitName) {

        if(fruitName.equalsIgnoreCase("strawberry")) {
            return new Strawberry();
        }
        else if(fruitName.equalsIgnoreCase("banana")) {

            return new Banana();
        }
        else {
            return null;
        }
    }
}
```

In the above code snippet, FruitFactory is an example for the following design pattern

a. Factory
b. Factory method
c. Abstract factory
d. None of the above

Ans: a

Answer Explanation:

Factory pattern is a creational pattern and objects are created using a common interface without exposing the creational logic to the client.

In the above sample, a client using the FruitFactory simply calls the getFruit() method passing the fruitName and the corresponding fruit object is returned.

9.1.5

```java
//Abstract Factory
public interface Fruit {

    void pick();
}

public class Strawberry implements Fruit {

    public void pick() {System.out.println("Pick strawberries");}
}

public class Banana implements Fruit {

    public void pick() {System.out.println("Pick a banana");}
}

public interface Milk {

    void pour();
}

public class Soymilk implements Milk {

    public void pour() {System.out.println("Pour soy milk");}
}

public class Almondmilk implements Milk {

    public void pour() {System.out.println("Pour almond milk");}
}
```

```java
public abstract class Smoothie {

    Fruit fruit;
    Milk milk;

    public abstract void makeSmoothie();
}

public class StrawberrySmoothie extends Smoothie {

    public StrawberrySmoothie(String smoothieName) {

        if(smoothieName.equalsIgnoreCase("strawberryDelight")) {

            fruit = new Strawberry();
            milk = new Almondmilk();
        }
        else {
            fruit = new Strawberry();
            milk = new Soymilk();
        }
    }

    public void makeSmoothie()  {

        System.out.println("Making strawberry smoothie");
    }
}

public class BananaSmoothie extends Smoothie {

    public BananaSmoothie(String smoothieName) {

        if(smoothieName.equalsIgnoreCase("bananaBonanza")) {

            fruit = new Banana();
            milk = new Almondmilk();
        }
        else {
            fruit = new Banana();
            milk = new Soymilk();
        }
    }
```

```java
    public void makeSmoothie() {

        System.out.println("Making banana smoothie");
    }
}

public interface AbstractSmoothieFactory {

    Smoothie getSmoothie(String smoothieName);
}

public class StrawberrySmoothieFactory implements
                            AbstractSmoothieFactory
{
    public Smoothie getSmoothie(String smoothieName) {

        return new StrawberrySmoothie(smoothieName);
    }
}

public class BananaSmoothieFactory implements
                            AbstractSmoothieFactory
{
    public Smoothie getSmoothie(String smoothieName) {

        return new BananaSmoothie(smoothieName);
    }
}

public class AbstractFactoryDemo {

    public static void main(String [] args) {

        AbstractSmoothieFactory bananaSf =
        AbstractFactoryDemo.getFactory("banana");

        Smoothie bananaSmoothie =
        bananaSf.getSmoothie("bananaBonanza");

        AbstractSmoothieFactory strawberrySf =
        AbstractFactoryDemo.getFactory("strawberry");
```

```
        Smoothie strawberrySmoothie =
        strawberrySf.getSmoothie("strawberryDelight");
    }
    public static AbstractSmoothieFactory getFactory(String
                                                    smoothieName)
    {
        AbstractSmoothieFactory sf = null;

        if(smoothieName.equalsIgnoreCase("banana")) {
            sf = new BananaSmoothieFactory();
        }
        else if(smoothieName.equalsIgnoreCase("strawberry")) {

            sf = new StrawberrySmoothieFactory();
        }
        else {
            return null;
        }
        return sf;
    }
}
```

The above sample of Abstract Factory pattern:

a. Is a creational pattern.
b. Provides interface for creating family of related objects.
c. Creates objects using object composition.
d. All of the above.

Ans: d

Answer Explanation:

Abstract factory is called factory of factories and creates other factories, so a creational pattern. In the above sample, StrawberrySmoothie Factory is a Abstract factory which in turn creates a Factory called StrawberrySmoothie.

In the above sample, getSmoothie(String smoothieName) is a Factory Method which is also a creational pattern.

The Factory method defines an interface and lets subclasses decide which class to instantiate. The objects are created using inheritance.

Abstract Factory as shown in the above sample often uses factory methods to implement the concrete factories.

9.1.6

Factory design pattern provides interface for creating a concrete class while Abstract Factory provides interface for creating a

a. Factory
b. Abstract Factory
c. Template method
d. None of the above

Ans: a

Answer Explanation:

Abstract factory is a factory of factories and creates other factories. Abstract Factory provides an interface for creating a family of related objects.

Each factory created in turn provides an interface for creating objects.

9.2 STRUCTURAL PATTERNS

9.2.1

```
//Adapter
public interface Jet {

    void takeOff();
    void land();
}

public class HelicopterAdapter implements Jet {

    Helicopter helicopter = null;

    public HelicopterAdapter(Helicopter helicopter) {

        this.helicopter = helicopter;
    }

    public void takeOff() { helicopter.rotateBlades(); }

    public void land() { helicopter.stop(); }
}
```

The above code snippet for an Adapter pattern

a. Is a structural pattern.
b. Converts interface of a class to another interface that the client expects.
c. Is a wrapper that changes the existing interface.
d. All of the above

Ans: d

Answer Explanation:

Adapter pattern is a structural pattern. Adapter pattern converts interface of a class to another interface that the client expects. Adapter allows classes to work together in spite of their incompatibilities. Adapter is a wrapper that changes the interface.

In the above example, a client that implements the Jet interface can use the HelicopterAdapter class. HelicopterAdapter class is a wrapper to Helicopter class and changes the Helicopter interface to be compatible with the Jet interface.

9.2.2

```
public class WakeupSleep {

    Alarm alarm;
    RoomLight light;
    RoomHeater heater;

    public void prepareToSleep() {

        alarm.on();
        light.off();
        heater.on();
    }

    public void prepareToWakeup() {

        alarm.off();
        light.on();
        heater.off();
    }
}
```

The above code snippet is an example for the following pattern:

a. Adapter
b. Facade
c. Decorator
d. Factory

Ans: b

Answer Explanation:

Facade pattern is a structural pattern and provides a simple and unified interface to the client by hiding complexities of the subsystem. Provides simplified methods that delegate calls to the subsystem methods.

WakeupSleep class provides two methods, prepareToSleep() and prepareToWakeup(). Within these two methods, the appropriate methods of the Alarm, RoomLight and RoomHeater classes are invoked, thus hiding the complexities and providing a simplified interface.

9.2.3

```java
//Decorator
public abstract class Cake {

    public abstract void getDetails();
}

public class MoltenChocolateCake extends Cake {

    public void getDetails() {

        System.out.println("Molten chocolate cake");
    }
}

public abstract class CakeDecorator extends Cake {

    public abstract void getDetails();
}

public class Frosting extends CakeDecorator {

    Cake cake;

    public Frosting(Cake cake) { this.cake = cake; }
```

```java
    public void getDetails() {
        cake.getDetails();
        System.out.println("Frosting");
    }
}
public class CandyMelt extends CakeDecorator {
    Cake cake;
    public CandyMelt(Cake cake) { this.cake = cake; }
    public void getDetails() {
        cake.getDetails();
        System.out.println("Candy melt");
    }
}
public static void main(String [] args) {
    Cake cake = new CandyMelt(new Frosting(new MoltenChocolateCake()));
    cake.getDetails();
}
```

The output for the above implementation of decorator pattern will be:

a. Molten chocolate cake, Frosting, Candy melt
b. Molten chocolate cake, Frosting
c. Molten chocolate cake, Candy melt
d. None of the above

Ans: a

Answer Explanation:

Decorator pattern is a structural pattern. Decorator adds new functionality to an existing object without altering its structure.

Decorator wraps the original class and provides additional functionality.

Output:

Molten chocolate cake
Frosting
Candy melt

In the above sample, Frosting and CandyMelt classes are both inherited from the CakeDecorator class which inherits the Cake class. A CakeDecorator class is a Cake class and also wraps a Cake class. This way, a Cake class can be decorated with any number of CakeDecorator classes as shown above.

9.2.4

Which of the following statement is true?

a. Adapter pattern converts one interface to another.
b. Decorator does not change the interface but adds functionality.
c. Facade simplifies the interface.
d. All of the above.

Ans: d

Answer Explanation:

Adapter wraps the original class and alters the interface. Decorator is also a wrapper, but adds functionality without changing the interface. Facade provides simplified interface for a set of subsystem classes.

9.2.5

public class BinaryTree {

    private Node root;

```
        private static class Node {

                int data;
                Node left;
                Node right;
                ----
        }
        ----
}
```

The above code snippet is an example for the following pattern

a. Adapter
b. Composite
c. Decorator
d. Facade

Ans: b

Answer Explanation:

Composite pattern composes objects into tree structures to represent part-whole hierarchies. It lets client treat individual objects and compositions of objects uniformly.

In the above BinaryTree class, the static inner class Node represents the Component which has the details to manage the child components.

A Node object with right and left nodes as null, but with a valid data value represents a leaf. A Node object with valid right and left nodes represents a Composite, which can have more child components.

The Composite pattern make clients simple, as the clients can treat the composite and individual objects uniformly.

9.3 BEHAVIORAL PATTERNS

9.3.1

public abstract class VeggieWrap {

    public final void prepare() {

        addVeggies();
        addCheese()
        wrap();
        addToPlate();
    }

    protected abstract void addVeggies();

    protected abstract void addCheese();

    public void wrap() { System.*out*.println("Wrapping");}

    public void addToPlate() { System.*out*.println("Adding to plate");}
}

public class AvocadoLettuceWrap extends VeggieWrap {

    protected void addVeggies() {

        System.*out*.println("Adding avocado, lettuce, and cucumber");
    }

    protected void addCheese() {

        System.*out*.println("Adding mozzarella cheese");
    }
}

The above class, defines skeleton of an algorithm in a method and defers some of the steps to the subclasses, this pattern is

a. Strategy

b. Template Method
c. Composite
d. Observer

Answer: b

Answer Explanation:

Template method pattern defines skeleton of an algorithm in a method and defers some of the steps to the subclasses. It's a behavioral pattern.

Template method pattern is used commonly after refactoring, as it allows code reuse from the base class and also allows the subclasses to specify the behavior.

In the above example, the prepare() method of abstract class VeggieWrap defines the skeleton of the algorithm to prepare a wrap by calling a few methods. Among the methods, addVeggies() and addCheese() are abstract methods that are implemented in the sub class AvocadoLettuceWrap.

9.3.2

```
public abstract class Airplane {

    Propeller propeller;
    Wing wing;

    public void takeOff() {

        propeller.start();
    }

    public void land() {

        wing.prepare();
    }

    public abstract void getDetails();
}
```

```java
public interface Propeller {

    void start();
}
public class TwoBladePropeller implements Propeller {

    public void start() {

        System.out.println("Preparing to start two blade propeller");
    }
}
public class ThreeBladePropeller implements Propeller {

    public void start() {

        System.out.println("Preparing to start three blade propeller");
    }
}
public interface Wing {

    void prepare();
}
public class LowWing implements Wing {

    public void prepare() {

        System.out.println("Preparing low wing");
    }
}
public class HighWing implements Wing {

    public void prepare() {

        System.out.println("Preparing high wing");
    }
}
```

```java
public class FighterPlane extends Airplane {

    public FighterPlane(Propeller propeller, Wing wing) {

        this.propeller = propeller;
        this.wing = wing;
    }

    public void getDetails() {

        System.out.println("FighterPlane with wing and propeller");
    }
}

public static void main(String [] args) {

    System.out.println("Invoking first FighterPlane ...");

    FighterPlane fp =
    new FighterPlane(new TwoBladePropeller(), new LowWing());

    fp.takeOff();
    fp.land();

    System.out.println("Invoking second FighterPlane ...");

    FighterPlane fp2 =
    new FighterPlane(new ThreeBladePropeller(), new HighWing());

    fp2.takeOff();
    fp2.land();
}
```

The above implementation is for a pattern that defines a family of algorithms, encapsulates them and makes them interchangeable. The pattern is

a. Strategy
b. Template Method
c. Composite
d. Observer

Answer: a

Answer Explanation:

Strategy defines a family of algorithms, encapsulates them and makes them interchangeable. Strategy design pattern is a behavioral pattern.

Strategy uses object composition and the algorithm implementation is handled by the composed objects.

In the above sample, Airplane class uses propeller and wing as composed objects. The algorithm implementation is done in the composed classes Propeller and Wing.

Multiple algorithms are available through the composed classes TwoBladePropeller, ThreeBladePropeller, LowWing, and HighWing and the client can choose any of them at runtime as shown in the main method.

9.3.3

Which of the following statement is true regarding Template Method and Strategy design pattern?

a. Template Method uses inheritance while Strategy uses object composition.
b. In Template Method, the algorithm structure is defined in the base class and details are deferred to the subclasses.
c. In Strategy, algorithm implementation is handled by the composed objects.
d. All of the above

Answer: d

Answer Explanation:

Template method design pattern defines skeleton of an algorithm in a method and defers some of the steps to the subclasses.

Strategy design pattern defines a family of algorithms, encapsulates them and makes them interchangeable.

9.3.4

```java
//Observer
import java.util.Observable;

public class GPSData extends Observable {

    private long distance;
    private long elevation;

    public long getDistance() { return distance; }

    public long getElevation() { return elevation; }

    public void updateChanges(long distance, long elevation) {

        System.out.println("GPSData - updating changes...");
        System.out.println("distance: " + distance + " elevation: " + elevation);

        this.distance = distance;
        this.elevation = elevation;
        //call Observable methods to notify changes to the Observers
        setChanged();
        notifyObservers();
    }
}

import java.util.Observable;
import java.util.Observer;

public class GPSDisplay implements Observer {

    Observable observable;
    private long distance;
    private long elevation;

    public GPSDisplay(Observable observable) {

        this.observable = observable;
        observable.addObserver(this);
    }
```

```java
    @Override
    public void update(Observable observable, Object arg) {

        if(observable instanceof GPSData ) {

            GPSData gpsData = (GPSData) observable;

            distance = gpsData.getDistance();
            elevation = gpsData.getElevation();

            displayChanges();
        }
    }

    public void displayChanges() {

        System.out.println("GPSDisplay - displaying distance...");
        System.out.println("distance: " + distance + " elevation: " + elevation);
    }
}

public static void main(String [] args) {

    GPSData gpsData = new GPSData();

    GPSDisplay gpsDisplay = new GPSDisplay(gpsData);
    gpsData.updateChanges(40, 3500);
}
```

In the above implementation of Observer pattern, the following method of the Observer gets called if the Observable updates the changes

a. displayChanges
b. setChanged
c. update
d. notifyObservers

Answer: c

Answer Explanation:

Observer pattern defines a one-to-many dependency between objects. When the observed object changes state, all the dependents get notified. Observer design pattern is a behavioral pattern.

Output for the above program is:

GPSData - updating changes...
distance: 40 elevation: 3500
GPSDisplay - displaying distance...
distance: 40 elevation: 3500

In main() method, GPSData and GPSDisplay objects are instantiated, gpsDisplay is the Observer object where the Observable object gpsData is set in the constructor.

When updateChanges() method on the gpsData is called, this method calls notifyObservers() method which in turn calls update() method on all the observers. The update() method of the GPSDisplay displays the changes.

9.3.5

```
public class Server extends Thread {

    static final int CAPACITY = 5;

    private BlockingQueue<Runnable> queue =
        new LinkedBlockingQueue<Runnable>(CAPACITY);

    public void accept(Runnable runnable) {

        queue.add(runnable); //producer
    }
    public void run() {

        while (true) {

            try {
                execute(queue.take()); //consumer
            }
```

```
            catch (InterruptedException e) {}
        }
    }

    private void execute(final Runnable runnable) {
        new Thread(runnable).start();
    }

    public static void main(String [] args) {
        Server server = new Server();

        server.accept(new Runnable() {
            public void run() {
                System.out.println("Executing task1");
            }
        });
        server.start();

        server.accept(new Runnable() {
            public void run() {
                System.out.println("Executing task2");
            }
        });
    }
}
```

The above Server class accepts Runnable objects as tasks to be executed. This is a Producer Consumer pattern, and also an example for the following pattern

a. Iterator
b. Composite
c. Command
d. Decorator

Ans: c

Answer Explanation:

Command design pattern enables requests to be saved and passed as objects. This is a behavioral pattern. It encapsulates requests in an object and allows saving requests in a queue. It decouples the receiver from the invoker.

In the above sample, the main() method creates two commands by calling server.accept() method for executing task1 and task2. The server.accept() method is called to pass the Runnable task which gets added to the queue. This is the producer that adds the task to the queue.

When server.start() is called, the run() method of the server class is invoked. This is the consumer thread that runs infinitely and takes the Runnable objects out of the queue and calls execute. A new thread is spawned in the execute() method to run each task.

Output:

Executing task1
Executing task2

9.3.6

```
public interface ElevatorState {

    public void goToFloor(int floorNumber);

    public void doorOpen();
    public void doorClose();
}

public class MovingUpState implements ElevatorState {

    Elevator elevator;

    public MovingUpState(Elevator elevator) {

        this.elevator = elevator;
    }

    public void goToFloor(int floorNumber) {
```

```java
            System.out.println("Moving up, cannot change destination");
        }

        public void doorOpen() {

            System.out.println("Moving up, cannot open door");
        }

        public void doorClose() {

            System.out.println("Moving up, cannot close door");
        }
    }

    public class StoppedOpenedState implements ElevatorState {

        Elevator elevator;

        public StoppedOpenedState(Elevator elevator) {

            this.elevator = elevator;
        }

        public void goToFloor(int floorNumber) {

            elevator.doorClose();
            elevator.setDestinationFloorNumber(floorNumber);

            if(floorNumber > elevator.getCurrentFloorNumber()) {

                elevator.setState(elevator.getMovingUpState());
            }
            else if(floorNumber < elevator.getCurrentFloorNumber()) {

                elevator.setState(elevator.getMovingDownState());
            }
        }

        public void doorOpen() {

            System.out.println("Door is already open");
        }
```

```java
    public void doorClose() {

        elevator.setState(elevator.getStoppedClosedState());
        System.out.println("Closing door");
    }
}

public class Elevator {

    ElevatorState movingUpState;
    ElevatorState movingDownState;
    ElevatorState stoppedOpenedState;
    ElevatorState stoppedClosedState;

    ElevatorState state = stoppedClosedState;

    int currentFloorNumber = 1;
    int destinationFloorNumber = 1;

    public Elevator() {

        movingUpState = new MovingUpState(this);
        movingDownState = new MovingDownState(this);
        stoppedOpenedState = new StoppedOpenedState(this);
        stoppedClosedState = new StoppedClosedState(this);
    }

    void setState(ElevatorState state) {
        this.state = state;
    }

    public void goToFloor(int floorNumber) {
        state.goToFloor(floorNumber);
    }

    public void doorOpen() {
        state.doorOpen();
    }

    public void doorClose() {
        state.doorClose();
    }
```

```java
    //getters and setters for instance variables
    public ElevatorState getMovingUpState() {
        return movingUpState;
    }
    public ElevatorState getMovingDownState() {
        return movingDownState;
    }

    public ElevatorState getStoppedOpenedState() {
        return stoppedOpenedState;
    }

    public ElevatorState getStoppedClosedState() {
        return stoppedClosedState;
    }

    public int getCurrentFloorNumber() {
        return currentFloorNumber;
    }

    public void setCurrentFloorNumber(int floorNumber) {
        this.currentFloorNumber = floorNumber;
    }

    public int getDestinationFloorNumber() {
        return destinationFloorNumber;
    }

    public void setDestinationFloorNumber(int floorNumber) {
        this.destinationFloorNumber = floorNumber;
    }

    //called once destination is reached
    public void reachedDestination() {
        //set currentFloorNumber
        currentFloorNumber = destinationFloorNumber;
        doorOpen();
    }
}
```

The above implementation of Elevator class using state pattern defines following number of states

a. four
b. five
c. two
d. three

Ans: a

Answer Explanation:

The state pattern is a behavioral pattern. It allows an object to alter its behavior when its internal state changes. The object will appear to change its class.

In the above sample, ElevatorState is an interface and represents the operational states through its methods. MovingUpState, MovingDownState, StoppedOpenedState and StoppedClosedState classes implement the ElevatorState class. Since the classes have similar functionalities only two of these state implementations are shown.

The Elevator class delegates all state specific operations to the corresponding state objects movingUpState, movingDownState, stoppedOpenedState and stoppedClosedState as shown.

As the state of the object changes, the corresponding state object is assigned to the member variable state of the Elevator class.

JVM Architecture

10.1 JVM BASICS

10.1.1

The term JVM refers to

a. the abstract specification
b. a concrete implementation
c. a run-time instance
d. all of the above

Ans: d

Answer Explanation:

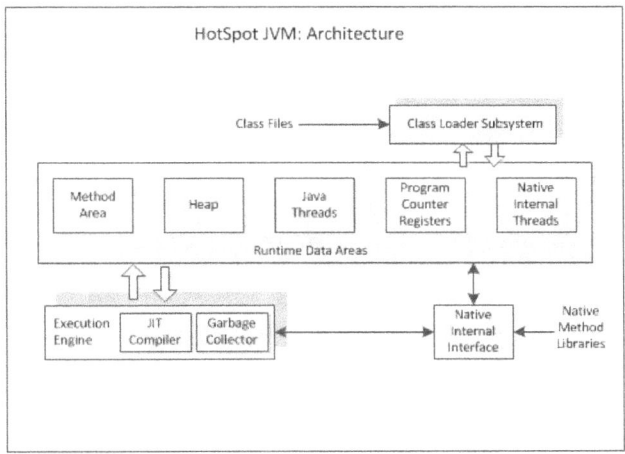

The term JVM may refer to the abstract specification as specified in the book "The Java Virtual Machine Specification" by Tim Lindholm and Frank Yellin or a concrete implementation available by various vendors in many platforms, which can be all software or a combination of hardware and software. A run-time instance hosts a single java application that is running.

Each java application runs inside the runtime instance, of a specific concrete implementation of the abstract specification of the java virtual machine. The job of a runtime instance of the java virtual machine is to run one java application.

JVM is a program which is like a machine to the programs that run on it. Each operating system has its own implementation of the JVM which translates the bytecode instructions into instructions that can work on the specific operating system.

10.1.2

If four java applications are started at the same time on the same computer, how many instances of java virtual machine are created?

a. one
b. two
c. four
d. zero

Ans: c

Answer Explanation:

When a java application starts, a runtime instance is born. When the application exits, the runtime instance dies. Each java application runs inside its own java virtual machine. The jvm starts running the application by invoking the main() method.

10.1.3

In the java virtual machine, the class loader subsystem is a mechanism for

a. loading classes
b. loading classes and interfaces
c. loading methods
d. None of the above

Ans: b

Answer Explanation:

Java applications are compiled into byte code stored in class files that are loaded into the JVM.

The part of the java virtual machine that handles finding and loading classes and interfaces is called the class loader subsystem.

10.1.4

In the java virtual machine, the execution engine is a mechanism for

a. executing instructions in the methods of the loaded classes
b. executing all instructions
c. executing byte codes
d. none of the above

Ans: a

Answer Explanation:

Execution engine in the JVM is a mechanism for executing the instructions in the methods of the loaded classes. The class loader loads the compiled java byte codes into runtime data areas and the execution engine executes the byte codes.

10.1.5

When the java virtual machine runs a program, it uses memory to store bytecodes, parameters to methods, return values, local variables and objects. The JVM organizes this memory into

a. heap
b. stack
c. register
d. runtime data areas

Ans: d

Answer Explanation:

The java virtual machine organizes the memory it needs to execute a program into runtime data areas.

The runtime data area has method area, heap, stacks, pc registers, and native method stacks. Some runtime data areas like method area and heap are shared by all threads of an application while some data areas like stacks and pc registers are unique to individual threads.

Local primitive variables like int, float etc. are pushed to the stack. Method parameters and return values are also pushed into the stack. Objects are stored in the heap.

10.1.6

The runtime data area has

a. method area and heap
b. pc register and stack
c. native method stacks
d. all of the above

Ans: d

Answer Explanation:

The runtime data area has method area, heap, stacks, pc registers, and native method stacks. Some runtime data areas like method area and heap are shared by all threads of an application while some data areas like stacks and pc registers are unique to individual threads.

10.1.7

The following areas are shared by all threads running inside the java virtual machine.

a. method area and heap
b. pc register and stack

c. runtime data area
d. none of the above

Ans: a

Answer Explanation:

Method area and heap are the two run time data areas that are shared by all threads.

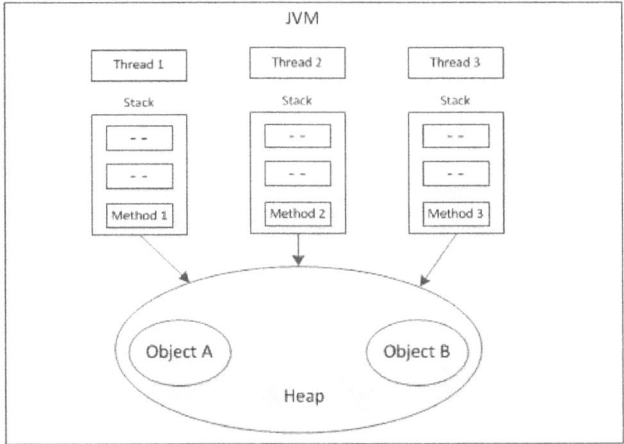

When the virtual machine loads the class files, it places the type information into the method area. The virtual machine places all objects into the heap.

10.1.8

In the java virtual machine, each new thread gets its own

a. method area and heap
b. pc register and stack
c. runtime data area
d. none of the above

Ans: b

Answer Explanation:

In the java virtual machine, each new thread gets its own pc register and stack.

When the thread is executing a java method, the pc register value has the next instruction to execute.

The thread's stack holds the state of the java method. The state of the java method includes the method parameters, its local variable, return values and intermediate calculated values.

10.1.9

Java classes in the java class path are loaded using the

a. bootstrap class loader
b. extension class loader
c. system class loader
d. secure class loader

And: c

Answer Explanation:

The class loader loads the compiled java classes into the java virtual machine.

The bootstrap class loader loads the core java classes like java.lang and java.util etc. The extension class loader loads the classes from the ext folder which are the extensions of the core java classes.

Classes in the java class path are loaded using the system class loader.

10.2 GARBAGE COLLECTION

10.2.1

The main garbage collection functionality is

a. automatic memory allocation
b. automatic memory deallocation
c. automatic memory allocation and deallocation
d. none of the above

Ans: b

Answer Explanation:

In programming languages like C and C++, memory allocation and deallocation is handled manually in the program. In Java, memory deallocation is automatically handled by the garbage collector.

During garbage collection, unreferenced objects are marked and then removed by the garbage collector.

10.2.2

Garbage collection mechanism is based on the analysis that

a. most objects are short lived
b. few objects are short lived
c. larger objects are short lived
d. smaller objects are short lived

Ans: a

Answer Explanation:

Analysis of data used in applications has shown that most of the objects allocated are short lived. This information is used for efficient garbage collection mechanism design.

The heap is broken up into three parts or generations called young generation, old or tenured generation, and permanent generation.

10.2.3

The heap is broken up into three parts or generations called

a. new generation, old or tenured generation and permanent generation.
b. young generation, old or tenured generation and permanent generation.
c. young generation, old or tenured generation and fixed generation.
d. none of the above

Ans: b

Answer Explanation:

All new objects are allocated and aged in the young generation. When young generation fills up a certain amount, this triggers a minor garbage collection as a result of which all the unreferenced objects are removed.

Since majority of the objects allocated are short lived, the young generation usually has large number of unreferenced objects that are cleaned.

All the minor garbage collection are stop the world events as all the application threads are stopped till this operation completes.

Some of the surviving objects are moved to the tenured generation as they age. The old generation stores long surviving objects. Old generation gets cleaned up by a process called major garbage collection.

Major garbage collection is also stop the world event but they happen less often and are also slower than minor garbage collection, since live objects are being handled.

GARBAGE COLLECTION

The permanent generation is used by the JVM to store metadata regarding classes and methods used in the application. This space is also cleaned by the garbage collector.

The young generation space is further divided into eden space, survivor space s0 and survivor space s1.

10.2.4

An object gets eligible for garbage collection when it is referenced only from a

a. HashMap
b. WeakHashMap
c. Array
d. ArrayList

Ans: b

Answer Explanation:

In the WeakHashMap, mappings that are not referenced outside the WeakHashMap are garbage collected.

When the garbage collector runs, it removes all the key/value pairs in the WeakHashMap that do not have a strong reference.

10.2.5

Difference between System.gc() and Object.finalize()

a. System.gc() can be invoked to call the garbage collector and garbage collector invokes the Object.finalize() method on unreferenced objects.
b. Object.finalize() is called when object goes out of scope which calls System.gc() to invoke the garbage collector.
c. System.gc() and Object.finalize get called by the JVM.
d. None of the above.

Ans: a

Answer Explanation:

System.gc() can be called explicitly to invoke the garbage collector but it is not guaranteed to run the garbage collector right away. It depends on the JVM implementation.

When an object is unreferenced, Object.finalize() method is called on the object by the garbage collector.

If there are any resources that need to be recycled or closed, the finalize() method cannot be relied. This is because the the time when the finalize() method will be called by the garbage collector cannot be determined. So, it's better to add a dispose() method in the code, to perform the cleanup and recycling of resources.

10.2.6

Memory leaks in Java happen when a program

a. keeps permanent reference to an object
b. keeps weak reference to an object
c. dereferences the objects that are not used
d. references objects in WeakHashMap

Ans: a

Answer Explanation:

Memory leaks happen when a program keeps a permanent reference to an object and the garbage collector cannot remove the object.

To avoid memory leaks, the object must be dereferenced by assigning the object to null when an object is no longer in use.

HashMap hMap = null;

Also when an object is no longer used, it should be dereferenced from static collections like HashMap and HashSet.

Thread local variables can also cause memory leaks, as they are similar to static variables. As threads are pooled and kept alive for long periods, the garbage collector will never get a chance to remove the thread local variables that are no longer in use.

Both static mutable variables and thread local variables should be used with caution as they can be major source for memory leaks.

www.ingramcontent.com/pod-product-compliance
Lightning Source LLC
Chambersburg PA
CBHW071914210526
45479CB00002B/409